Looking, Listening and Learning: Observing and Assessing Young Readers

Observing and Assessing Young Readers

Looking, Listening, and Learning

by Carl Braun

97 96 95 94 93 5 4 3 2 1

Canadian Cataloguing in Publication Data

Braun, Carl

Looking, listening, and learning

Includes bibliographical references.

ISBN 1-895411-55-6

1. Reading (Elementary)—Evaluation. 2. Reading (Elementary)—Ability testing. 3. Observation (Educational method). I. Title.

LB1050.46.B72 1993 372.4'076 C93-098075-1

Acknowledgments
Figure 4.1—Reprinted from *Literacy Profiles Handbook: Assessing and Reporting* by courtesy of the Department of School Education, Victoria, Australia.

Figures 4.2, 4.3, 4.4, 7.3 ©1990; figures 5.2, 7.4 ©1989—From Strategies by C. Braun & P. Goepfert. Used by permission of Nelson Canada. A division of Thomson Canada.

Book and cover design: Pat Stanton

Printed and bound in Canada by Hignell Printing Limited

Peguis Publishers
520 Hargrave Street
Winnipeg, Manitoba
Canada R3A 0X8

Contents

II. OBSERVATION AND ASSESSMENT IN PRACTICE

FIGURES

Editor's Note

One of the dilemmas facing today's editor is that of retaining writing clarity while ensuring gender balance. This relates specifically to the use of the personal pronouns he/she, him/her, himself/herself, and so on. Using both forms in all cases makes for particularly awkward reading. In this book we have chosen to use masculine pronouns in reference to students and feminine pronouns in reference to teachers. We assure the reader that no affront is intended in any way.

Preface

Most of us were schooled in a tradition that recognized the teacher as the paragon of knowledge and control. Children looked and listened; teachers directed children to look and listen; they told children where to look and what to look for. We still believe that learners must know where to look and how to listen. But this includes all learners, even teachers, or should I say *especially* teachers. This book is about teachers observing children, looking and listening to discover new insights into children's learning. It is also about the need to learn more about our own practices of observation and instruction of children and then to listen and look inside ourselves. It highlights the need to bring assessment, learning, and instruction into alignment.

This view is at war with the widely held perception that literacy reform must begin by tightening controls on schools and that the instruments of control reside in assessment schemes designed and dictated by people beyond the school borders. In Part One I argue that externally imposed assessment agendas constrain what teachers and children do in classrooms—how teachers teach and how children learn. Ultimately such control strips teachers of their professional dignity and limits teacher change. Alternatively, I present the view that assessment that accords teachers and children center stage has the potential for ongoing learning, positive teacher change, and long-term educational change. That is, day-to-day observation and assessment that center on children's learning rather than on tests not only inform instruction, they also lead to new ways of looking and listening. Teachers will learn more about children and about their own learning and teaching. Contrary to the traditional view, which sees learning, teaching, and assessment as discrete entities, the approach taken here is that assessment, learning, and instruction form an integral whole as children and teachers collaborate.

Part Two addresses practical issues about observation and assessment. I begin with a discussion of classroom learning environments and how these environments shape positive feelings and attitudes toward reading. Observation of the emergent reader takes on special prominence as I integrate many of Marie Clay's landmark observations about young children's learning with observations I have made in my own classroom and clinical work with young children over the past four decades. As we learn to extend our gaze in observing the emergent reader, we learn to appreciate what children bring to the school literacy experience, enabling a more natural transition from home to school. At the same time, we can prevent many of these children from creating "tangles," which in the past have resulted in long-term frustration and failure. We can, through astute observation, help children develop learning strategies that move them toward the development of fluency and confidence.

Finally, I discuss observation of readers who have already "emerged" (though the line is arbitrary). I emphasize the importance of teachers and children monitoring together as they listen, as they interpret running records, as they expand their ways of looking, listening, and learning. Again, it is my belief that as we observe children we must continually monitor our own observation, our own learning. That is what change is all about. That is what lifelong learning is about.

It is my hope that, whether you are a teacher of young children or a student at a college or university aspiring to join the ranks of teachers of young children, you are able to capture or recapture a sense of optimism and a sense of confidence as a learner as you read this book. Above all, my sincere wish for all is that you share the excitement and joy that come from listening to children, watching them, and learning from them each day.

I thank Winnifred, my daughter, a parent and teacher whose eager looking and listening continue to challenge my own observations of children's learning. Her sensitivities continue to inspire me to listen and look in new ways. I acknowledge with pleasure the many children who through the years have given me opportunities to listen, look, and learn. These children, in classrooms, in smaller groups, or in individual settings, have been my teachers —in the best sense of the word. The lessons I've learned go back to the children I taught in the one-room school in the early fifties, and the elementary, junior, and senior high-school students I taught in the mid-sixties. I remember the lessons well, though they have been filtered through layers and layers of new learning. I thank the children who even today trust me enough to learn with me. Finally, I thank the many students and practicing teachers from whom I continue to learn, and who continue to make learning so enjoyable—even after my pretence at retirement. From Vancouver to Pictou County in Nova Scotia, I have such a wealth of co-learners, many of whom have become lifelong friends. How could I ever thank them enough!

Introduction

Oscar, a nine-year old child, lives in a family that through economic circumstances has moved three times in the past six months. During this period, Oscar has had instruction by an ESL teacher, one-on-one instruction by a resource teacher, and "intensive reading instruction" in a learning disabilities classroom.

Four weeks ago Oscar was enrolled at Westbrooke Meadows School. His placement in a regular grade-three classroom was seen as a temporary measure. In the meantime he has been given a series of tests to determine "optimum placement" in his new school setting. The results suggest that he could qualify for funding for special class placement. His "language capacity," especially in the areas of syntactic fluency and vocabulary, place him in the "low normal" range. His reading comprehension and word reading knowledge place him in the second and third stanines, respectively. At a conference, the language specialist, resource teacher, and psychologist concluded that Oscar would best be served by placement in a special class until he "picks up the language and develops basic reading skills."

There is one loud dissenting voice that initially is seen as a kind of nuisance; a voice that contradicts what "seems like very straightforward evidence." Jan Monash, Oscar's classroom teacher, has done with Oscar what she does with all children in her charge. She has observed him in all kinds of settings and has created every opportunity for Oscar to feel comfortable in his new setting. What is more, she goes into the conference anticipating the kind of decision-making she has seen once too often. She is armed with conference notes, recordings of Oscar's participation in discussions, recordings of his reading with

> a range of supports, and samples of his writing. At the conference table, Jan sees herself as an advocate for Oscar; her observations not only refute every shred of evidence *against* Oscar (as she interprets the fragmented test results), but demonstrate "beyond the shadow of a doubt that Oscar is a very capable child." Further, she declares with gusto, her observations point clearly to "some of the kinds of instruction that Oscar benefits from." One of her concerns about changes in placement, at this point, is that Oscar has begun to make friends with some children in the class, much to the delight of both Oscar and his parents. There simply is too much at stake, Jan contends, and for the wrong reasons.

Unlike many stories with similar beginnings, the Oscar story has a happy ending. Oscar remains in Jan's class, and he is achieving far beyond even Jan's initial expectations. As Jan says, "Not only is Oscar surviving, he has so much to contribute to the class. He is becoming a star in his own right. Give him another three months, and Oscar will be not only one of the best readers, but also the most avid. What an asset to the class!"

Jan has tremendous confidence in her abilities as a teacher, fanned liberally with exceptional beliefs in the capabilities of children. She is an outstanding observer of children. Not only does she listen, she hears; not only does she look, she sees. Those striking attributes, combined with an administrator whose belief in Jan supersedes beliefs in paper-and-pencil evidence, are changing Oscar's life—forever! What power! What a challenge!

Recent interest in alternative forms of assessment, interest in day-to-day observation as an alternative to some of the practices of the past, has led to wide debate. More and more, teachers are beginning to experience the liberation for both themselves and children that comes from tightening the ties between *what* they see and hear as they teach, and *how* they will teach.

What Do We Mean by Observation?

Classroom observation of children has sometimes been referred to as *kid watching*, and that is likely a good descriptor for what classroom observation is all about. This watching is motivated and maintained by interest and excitement in what is happening in the child's world of learning and development. Kid watching is not just for teachers, although initially they are the expert observers and watchers. Children, to achieve their potential as learners, become keen observers as well—of their own learning and the learning of their peers. That is all part of an effective learning environment.

There is another category of partners in observation—the parents. They are, after all, the first observers, and observers with a strong stake in the overall learning development of their child. It is in the child's best interests that the school respect parents' continuing involvement in the process of kid watching.

Observation should never be perceived as police or detective work. Observing in the classroom, or wherever there are children, simply implies wide-open, interested eyes and ears. Through our eyes and ears we observe the day-to-day growth and refinements in learning that take place. Sometimes we observe major breakthroughs or mini-revolutions in a child's learning. At other times we see plateaus—times when the child is settling into a repertoire of new understandings. Recognition of these settling-in learning points is as important as recognition of the "aha" breakthroughs. Still at other times a child appears, to the uneducated observer, to regress. In fact the current stage may be part of a larger settling-in, sorting-out process, critical to long-term learning development.

Observation has to do with keeping track of what is going on with each child's learning. This process is as varied as the talents and idiosyncracies of each child, the individual styles and beliefs of teachers, and the learning environments of the child's world. The process is not one of passive looking and listening. It is active. At the risk of oversimplifying I will give a few examples.

You only have to read the introductory paragraph of a piece or opening chapter of a book with the child to determine whether knowledge of the overall context leads to enhanced fluency. Observation may involve asking a child to listen to a recording of his own oral reading to learn what suggestions he has for improvement, and then to see whether or not he has the kinds of strategies necessary to make these modifications. It may involve reading a piece of the child's own writing to him to see if the distance created by an outside reader leads to revisions not apparent from his own reading of his work. The range of observations, then, is limited by the teacher's creative resources, and even more so, by time constraints.

Observation is the key to learning. The more one learns (this goes for both children and teachers), the more one is competent to see and hear. Observation is looking, listening, being part of the learning.

Exploring Assessment Agendas

I

Why Observation Is So Critical to Successful Child Learning

1

Highlighting Children's Learning and Fine-tuning Instruction

We observe children in our classrooms partly because we are interested in *how* they learn. In a sense we are as curious about their learning as they are curious about the world around them. But there's more to it than that. What we observe about the child's day-to-day learning informs us of the kinds of curriculum modifications needed to broaden that learning. These observations, on the one hand, help us to fine-tune instruction, and on the other, to fine-tune our ability to observe.

Observation is a learned ability. It comes from knowledge of child development and learning, which in turn is learned through interaction with and observation of children. The finer the tuning, the more discoveries we make about the child's learning achievements and his potential to go further. There is no doubt that children's learning is enhanced immeasurably by the teacher's ability and openness to hear and see. Oscar's teacher, Jan, is a prime example of a teacher who possesses these qualities.

Ongoing observation, then, has an important preventative function. If children, especially in the early stages of reading and writing, are expected to proceed in lock-step fashion with other children, they are far more likely to drift into narrow strategies. This is far more limiting than facilitative—especially in circumstances where pressure to compete is pervasive, and observation is, at best, haphazard. Clay places the matter of prevention into context: "The difficulties of the young child might be more easily overcome if he had practiced error less often, had less to unlearn and relearn, and still had reasonable confidence in his ability" (1985: 10). Prevention is our best defense.

FLAGGING FLEDGLING STRATEGIES TO FAN THE LEARNING SPARK

Traditionally most observation/assessment energies focused on detecting difficulties and documenting "missing skills." We know today that it is much more productive to highlight learning strategies that are there and then help the child build on these. And the greater the skill of the observer, the greater the inventory of strategies children are going to be credited with. That is why the best teachers, especially those of young children, are the most astute observers of children. These teachers enable children to recognize the strategies they are using effectively and then encourage them to refine and use the strategies till they become automatic. They help children to see and understand what they are doing *right* and what they can do to move forward.

Tanya, for example, has learned through her experiences with books to follow memorized text by moving her finger along word for word as she reads. Her teacher recognizes that Tanya has learned an extremely important strategy—one that demonstrates she already understands the rudiments of the abstract relationship among the squiggles on the pages, the sounds that she makes, and meaning. Tanya is not examining text in any critical way. At this point she is not even taking note of the print features—word form, letters, and so forth. She is mapping text word for word, a much more sophisticated strategy than is often recognized. Her teacher knows that Tanya should be encouraged to continue using this strategy. She knows that eventually Tanya will move to the point where she notices beginnings of words, endings of words, similarities, and differences. Right now Tanya has a looking and listening strategy that allows her to move toward strategies in which she makes analogies about words in text she enjoys.

The distinction between what was popularly referred to as "skills" and the more current concept of "strategies" is a less than subtle one, a distinction that holds important implications for both observation and instruction. *Skills* have typically been seen as accumulations or inventories of "pieces" of knowledge. For example, the child might know beginning consonants, a given repertoire of sight words, or long vowel words ending in *e*. *Learning strate-*

gies are the means by which children learn how to learn, the ways of making new knowledge from what is currently being learned. For example, the child learns that the sound he hears at the beginning of his name is the same as the beginning sound of his favorite cereal or the name of a friend. He learns that these sounds are typically represented in print by the same letter, knowledge that he can apply whenever he hears words that begin with the same sound. He has a strategy that he can apply to other words that he hears and sees—one that holds not only for words that begin the same as his name but for other words as well. He has a strategy for making analogies from what he hears and sees. A further example: the child discovers that rhymes he has learned have words with endings that not only sound the same but also use the same or similar letter endings. Again, he has learned more than the words *Jill* and *hill;* he has learned something about the writing system that he can apply to new instances of rhyme. Clay (1991) refers to the development of self-extending, self-generative learning, rather than the learning of "inventories of items."

Children who are in skills programs *do* learn strategies that are self-generative, and teachers who see skills as the goal of instruction *do* point children (at least incidentally) in the direction of strategy learning. But the overall goals of learning and instruction are different in skills and strategies classrooms; the landmarks for observation are radically different as are the degrees of complexity of observation. For the child, the inclination to learn is critically shaped by the orientation of the teacher—either toward skills or strategies learning.

There are many children like Tanya whose fledgling strategies need only to be encouraged. But that requires that we know how to listen and what to look for.

DETECTING COUNTERPRODUCTIVE STRATEGIES EARLY

While one of the prime purposes of classroom observation is to identify a child's learning assets and to build on these, there are children who come to school with flawed notions about learning—especially about learning to read and write. These notions may run the gamut, from beliefs that reading is a mechanical process in which meaning is secondary, to beliefs that spitting out isolated sounds achieves fluency and that unconstrained guessing at words results in successful reading. Some children, indeed too many, find themselves in snags and tangles, which left undetected, result in failure. As Clay has put it, the more children with limiting strategies practice the wrong things, the harder they try; then the tangles become greater. These children are not developing self-improving strategies. Unless they are fortunate enough to have a teacher who understands children's learning—one who knows what to observe, one who is able to help the child to develop new strategies—these children are at risk.

Following are some examples of the kinds of snags that children frequently encounter that often go undetected.

A child may be asked to pay attention to specific aspects of print—beginning sounds, words, parts (syllables), and so on—long before he understands the general nature of print: the one-to-one match between spoken and written language. Such knowledge is prerequisite to knowing where to look, how to look, what to listen for. Frequently children are asked to give attention to specific parts of words—beginnings, endings, vowels, consonants—before they even understand the distinction among words, letters, sentences, and so on. Often children find themselves in mazes of print long before they have a sense of where to begin on the page, or in what direction to move their eyes. The harder the teacher teaches, and the harder the child tries to follow the lessons on specific "skill bits" in such circumstances, the greater the potential for long-term frustration, abandonment, and failure.

To highlight this critical concern, I provide a vignette of a young learner who through expert observation was given a chance at just the right time.

> Brian had been in school for three years. Exceptionally bright, he had a wealth of knowledge and an excellent command of English. By the beginning of grade three, however, Brian was beginning to engage in all sorts of non-productive behavior. His reading skills were at best rudimentary.
>
> A student who had begun to work with Brian recorded a short reading selection. Brian read it haltingly, substituting numerous nonsensical words. The student quickly rewrote the passage, transcribing the words in random order. She asked Brian to read the jumbled passage. The reading of this version was no better than the reading of the first. Brian listened to the reading of the latter version, commenting only after he had listened to half of his reading that it didn't make sense. The ensuing discussion disclosed that this was the first time that Brian had ever considered that reading should make sense—knowledge that *any* reader must have.

Brian is a classic case of a child engaged in non-productive reading behavior—behavior that could only lead to further frustration and long-term failure. But the first-class observation strategies used by the student teacher led not just to fine-tuning of instruction, but to dramatic rerouting of instruction and an equally dramatic turnabout in learning. Brian now has what Clay calls self-improving, self-sustaining strategies. Brian now knows when things aren't working and has a means by which he is able to monitor his own learning. He can either "fix things" on his own or ask for assistance. Meaning is the overall criterion for this monitoring. And when meaning fails, Brian knows it. He is no longer in the dark. That doesn't mean that all his problems have been solved. It *does* mean, however, that the path has been cleared for him to move in productive directions. All this because of one teacher's ability to use perceptive, intelligent eyes and ears.

The implications of professional observation in cases like Brian's go far beyond helping the learner to "patch up" achievement difficulties, as important as that is. The spinoffs are social and emotional for the Brians of the world as well as for their families. Kemp, among others, has documented the terrible stress placed on families in which children persist with learning problems that go undetected by the school, and when detected, unremedied. He found that families were often aware of problems long before the school reported evidence of such problems. Even after the problems were detected, most parents waited for two years before some action was taken, some as long as five and six years.

Both lack of expertise and time pressures have contributed to the inability of teachers to detect counterproductive strategies of children and have kept them from taking action. What needs to be underlined in any case is that social and emotional pressures take their toll in very short order—not only at school but at home. Kemp reported this to be the case for over half the families he had interviewed. Parents reported that singling out one child for special help, for instance, caused other family members to be envious and demanding. Parents felt guilt and feared "receiving the next report." Some reported "constant anxiety and conflict" not only between parents and children but also between parents. One reported, "Our marriage has nearly fallen to pieces because of him"; another, "My husband goes berserk; the whole family is on a tightrope when the homework gets out" (1987: 28-29).

In short, children often become marginalized socially both at home and at school because of problems that could and should have been dealt with earlier. In many instances, these problems could have been averted through reasonable professional observation and appropriate instruction. Again I am arguing for preventative action. (If the public, especially politicians and administrators, understood even vaguely the savings in human dignity and long-term economics, teacher support, pre-service and inservice education, and deployment of resources would be revolutionized immediately.)

SCOUTING FOR LEARNER POTENTIAL

I believe that one of the attributes that separates excellence from mediocrity in teaching is the ability to spot potential in just about anything that children say or do. Seeing potential before the learner even suspects potential is the mark of a truly great observer, a great teacher.

The astute teacher-observer is in a prime position to catch the signs of a child's potential that neither parent nor child has suspected. The more observant the teacher, the greater the chance that the child will have these sparks of potential recognized—and fanned. Further, the greater the resourcefulness of the teacher and the richer the learning context, the greater the opportunities for children to demonstrate a wide range of competencies and potential. The narrower the context, the fewer opportunities there are to demonstrate what is possible. The more restricted the teacher's gaze, the greater the chance that potential will go undetected. What a responsibility for the teacher! Conversely, what an exciting, grand opportunity! Again, I resort to an example:

> Salina, a seven-year-old, had considerable difficulty reading and writing. What was more, she had already learned to regard herself as a failure. One of her teacher's biggest challenges was to engage Salina in reading and writing tasks with any kind of spark or confidence. One day during recess the teacher noted that Salina had a tremendous repertoire of skipping rhymes and songs, many in the English language, some in her native tongue. Salina chanted these with a remarkable sense of rhythm. The teacher did no more at this point than make mental notes. She just kept watching and listening for more. One day during a conference with Salina, the teacher commented on Salina's knowledge of chant and song. Salina was delighted. The teacher asked Salina to start putting some of her pieces on tape. One of her parents became involved in the project as well. The teacher, with aid of an interpreter from another class, transcribed them as part of Salina's reading materials. The success, of course, was almost instant. Furthermore, Salina discovered an ability to use some of the existing rhythmic scaffoldings to compose her own verse.

There are many demonstrations of scouting of this sort that go on every day. Teachers and administrators need to recognize these events as evidence of true professional greatness. Scouting for potential, communicating this potential, and then assisting the young learner to capitalize on it, promise to develop confidence in self and ultimately new energy to pursue new learnings and to refine and extend existing strategies. Observation is critical!

COLLECTING DATA FOR EFFECTIVE REPORTING

Reporting on children's learning has long been the bane of teachers everywhere. Problems of what to report, how to report, how frequently, and to whom are only some of the knotty issues linked to reporting.

Traditionally reports on children's learning have often consisted of lists of skills that children have mastered in a given period of time. These lists usually fall short of providing a comprehensive picture of the young learner, and have been limited to the skills and behaviors observable by the myopic, or at least, untrained eye.

Wide observation, on a day-to-day basis and in a wide range of learning contexts, provides a sound basis for painting a comprehensive picture of the learner. Rather than reporting "Sam knows his upper-case letters, and must spend time learning his lower-case letters" (something that any person on the street could observe), a report should reflect on strategies Sam is coming to terms with and on the instruction that is being provided to help him build on these strategies.

DETERMINING FUNCTIONAL LINKS BETWEEN LEARNING AND INSTRUCTION

Johnston (1992) makes a plea for the need to wed assessment/observation to learning and instruction. Day-to-day observation makes that kind of wedding possible. To put this generalization into context, I share with you some critical incidents from the educational experiences of Maurice, who in the span of six months, encountered some of the extremes of a traditional approach to assessment, an approach quite consciously and blatantly isolated from instruction (and as you will see, quite unrelated to subsequent learning). While Maurice at age nine was older than children who would normally be identified as emergent readers and writers, he was in the most critical sense not "emerging." He was stuck.

Maurice had a history of failure. Finally, in grade three, he was referred for a "full-scale" assessment. The reason cited: his "performance in the language arts was below expectations for his grade level." The psychologist's report revealed that Maurice was well above average intellectually, a finding of no great surprise to his parents. The resource teacher administered a series of standardized diagnostic tests and an assortment of system-wide word analysis and spelling tests. The conclusion: "Maurice is seriously deficient in word attack and has no comprehension."

The results of the assessment led to a fairly predictable program of remediation—concentrated work in word analysis, extensive work on short comprehension passages, and an exhortation to read high-interest, low vocabulary books at home. That Maurice did not have a reading vocabulary to deal with the "comprehension" passages never entered the picture. Nor did the fact that Maurice had long given up hope of learning to read and write.

Maurice remained in his new remedial program for the next four months (until the end of the school term). He was pulled from the classroom for tutorials once a day. His lack of progress at the end of the term was attributed to "lack of effort to invest energy in the program."

That summer Maurice and his family moved to another part of the community. His family expressed surprise when Maurice's new teacher showed little interest in the report he had brought from the previous school. They were mildly surprised when they discovered that she was not about to blindly plug in to the prescribed program that had failed the previous term. She told the parents that she needed time to work with Maurice and that he, in turn, needed time to feel comfortable with her and his new peers. Maurice's teacher observed him closely to discover not so much what he wasn't able to do but more what he was capable of doing, so that she and Maurice could identify strategies that must be extended for new learning.

The teacher continued to make diary entries about observations (as she did with other children in the classroom). She noted that Maurice had a wealth of experience and knowledge about many things. She observed Maurice in a variety of instructional situations and noted how he responded to this instruction. Reluctantly at first, but with zeal and energy after he discovered that it was safe, Maurice contributed significantly to class discussion and to group projects.

There were many short conferences, mostly spontaneous. One of these, involving a talk about Maurice's reading of a short, taped selection, resulted in the following comments in the teacher's diary:

> "Maurice dislikes reading. He has no idea that reading should make sense and as a result does not make use of the rich resource of ideas he has to make reading easier. He has a limited inventory of isolated skills which do not work for him. He puts together a few simple statements on paper, but makes no attempt to use his wide knowledge to create something interesting. He is so preoccupied with indenting and correct spelling that this seems to take all the energy he is willing or able to invest in writing.
>
> "I am finding interesting pieces for Maurice to read and I am getting him involved in reading and writing with some of the other kids. He is taping his reading from time to time so that he can listen to it. Then we talk about the things that he is doing well, things that can be changed, and even more important, what he can do to change. Yes, Maurice needs to know that there are many things he is already doing right and that he has the ability to develop strategies that will enable him to continue improving. What he needs more than anything else is success, and he needs it now. I must listen and observe and see how he can become involved most beneficially with the group and get Maurice to contribute to the class in meaningful ways. This will mean that he has to trust us all enough to risk being wrong. I think he is going to be happy here." (Adapted from Braun and Goepfert 1989: 8.)

Maurice's teacher believes that ongoing observation of children's learning provides the only reasonable window to the child's learning *and* to her instruction. Observing as she is teaching provides part of the assessment information she needs to make adjustments to instruction and materials. Observing Maurice while he is interacting with other children provides another vital part of the comprehensive learning picture. She realizes that a child's performance varies from one time to another, and observing learning in varied contexts provides the necessary clues to how the learning environment should be structured (or unstructured). In short, observation happens all the time, just as learning and instruction happen all the time. The unprofessional observer will not be able to differentiate which, assessment or instruction, is the key focus as the two are so intimately intertwined. This does not mean that the teacher won't occasionally structure a task expressly for the purpose of observing a particular aspect of the child's learning. This is sometimes necessary to get a clearer window on successful learning strategies *and* a clearer vision of how to fine-tune instruction at a particular time in the child's learning history.

In summary, two points must be emphasized. First, teachers like Maurice's recognize that to obtain a true window on learning, children need to feel the freedom to take risks. For example the questions a child asks when he wants clarification may be among the most important information the teacher is presented with on any given day. The practice of observation integrated with daily learning and teaching routine creates freedom for the child. It completely eliminates the notion that "this is testing time; I better be careful." "Being too careful" in a formal assessment context creates blinkered vision. It limits the information available to the teacher's view. Second, teachers need to recognize that the data that guides instruction comes out of credible tasks rather than contrived, trivial traps designed to catch the child being wrong. Useful observational data comes from real invitations to learn. Observational data such as that derived by Maurice's teacher then, creates a highly functional link between learning and instruction. In Maurice's case it went further. It created social links, and more important, retrieved Maurice from the mire of learned helplessness.

ATTRIBUTING SUCCESS TO LEARNER STRATEGIES

We hear much about learner empowerment these days. We hear less about how to provide environments that promote this.

Much of what Maurice's teacher did in her day-to-day observation and instruction laid the foundation for Maurice's long-term empowerment. Both teacher and child took careful account of instruction and those strategies that resulted in significant learning on Maurice's part. Knowing what "I can do to help myself" is the essence of empowerment. Knowing why something worked and something else did not goes a long way in enabling learners to find their own way and to continue on a productive course.

Children who are invited to share the secrets of their learning are more likely to progress than those for whom the secrets—at one time the domain of the teacher—remain hidden. Children who are taught early that self-monitoring is part of their responsibility as learners are more likely to advance quickly than those who are dependent on the teacher's next dictates. They are more likely to explore, take risks, and become responsible for their own learning than those who are tightly linked to the teacher's instructional prescription.

More specifically, these children are soon able to make statements about needed adjustments in learning environments that result in improved learning for them. The following statements show clearly how children use their knowledge to propel their own learning:

I am going to tape this so that I can tell how it sounds. Then I can make changes.

If I read this with a partner first, I think I can do it on my own.

This word rhymes with platter; *the word must be* matter.

I know that I am missing periods and things. I'll ask Janet to read my piece to me, and then I will know where to put the marks.

I know I didn't read my part often enough. It's not smooth. It's too bumpy. I'll take it home and read it often.

Child-teacher discussion about attribution of success in learning is one of the keys to the child's control over his own learning. Knowing *why* he is successful and being aware of the conditions under which he is developing critical learning strategies free him from constant dependence on expert guidance and advice. This is important not only for long-term success as a reader but for success as a learner, generally.

Concluding Comments

Ongoing kid watching—creative teacher observation—is the key to successful learning experiences for children and for teachers. As teachers see ongoing observation as an integral part of teaching, they put themselves in an ongoing learning situation. In other words, ongoing observation of children is the best guarantee that the teacher will be an ongoing learner.

This interaction with children and the continuing reflection about children and learning are what take "kid watchers" to the pinnacle of professionalism. This makes possible that critical marriage of assessment/observation, learning and instruction. As Peter Johnston so wisely said, it is the teacher who becomes the fine-tuned assessment instrument.

Ongoing, intelligent observation is a proactive move on behalf of children. It is driven by the belief that taking preventative action makes more sense than waiting for children to flounder, and then trying to extricate them from their learning problems—which are so often intensified by low self-esteem. Day-to-day observation provides a framework for learning and instruction and invites on-the-spot adjustments. It lays the foundations for the integration of existing strategies and points the way to new strategies. It is simply intelligent investment in the lives of children, in the life of a nation.

REFERENCES

Braun, C., and P. Goepfert. *Swinging Below a Star.* In Strategies. Scarborough, ON: Nelson Canada, 1989.

Clay, M. M. *Detecting Reading Difficulties.* Portsmouth, NH: Heinemann, 1985.

———. *Becoming Literate: The Construction of Inner Control.* Portsmouth, NH: Heinemann, 1991.

Johnston, P. H. *Constructive Evaluation of Literate Activity.* New York: Longman, 1992

Kemp, M. *Watching Children Read and Write: Observational Records for Children with Special Needs.* Portsmouth, NH: Heinemann, 1987.

Assessing Readers in the Nineties: Changing Perspectives

2

The eighties and nineties have opened up critical debates about how assessment/observation should be done. While somewhat oversimplified, two views on assessment have emerged: traditional and child-centered. The traditional view focuses on observation of the child's skill development. Generally speaking, this view is grounded in a psychometric framework—the belief that learning is sequential, measurable, and quantifiable. The current view, variously referred to as ecological assessment or child-centered observation, takes a much more inclusive view of the child's learning.

In this chapter I outline basic philosophical differences between traditional and child-centered views on assessment/observation, and look at current issues surrounding the observation of young children's reading. As I do so, I point out practical differences that spring from these newer perspectives. After all, it is only when children's learning is enhanced that such differences have any importance for teachers. I should also point out that what I call new is relative. Much of what I say here has been said by others in the past five or six years. Some frameworks that I propose are new, however—as are some of the practical applications that I suggest.

Traditionally we have been concerned with indexing inventories of children's skills. Instruction was focused on helping the child fill the gaps assumed as a result of the assessment. Child-focused observation is concerned more with *how* children use strategies to solve day-to-day reading and writing problems and the resources the child has for solving these problems. The teacher can then move in to help children build on these resources.

The following views of traditional and current approaches to assessment should help teachers understand ways to maximize children's abilities through the evolution of different ways of seeing and hearing. (Please note: While a bipolar system of discussion helps to achieve clarity, it also runs the risk of oversimplification. I am taking that risk with the caution that some of the differences between the two views may be more a matter of degree than absolute, though certainly they are driven by quite diverse beliefs about children and learning.)

Examining Alternate Assessment Perspectives

OBSERVATION PROVIDES LINKS TO INSTRUCTION

In traditional assessment, educators believed that test results showed where skill deficits lay. The link between actual instruction and observations was a prescriptive one: that is, those who lacked Skill A received instruction in Skill A. It was assumed, of course, that the result of the assessment was a reliable and valid guide to instructional needs. The perceived links between observation and instruction were quite reasonable given prevailing views about children's learning and instruction. After all, these views were firmly entrenched in a diagnostic/prescriptive tradition analogous to that of the medical tradition. To illustrate, it makes sense that a diagnosis of leukemia be followed with a prescription for appropriate treatment. The analogy breaks down in education, however. The child, for example, who is "weak in producing consonant blends" is unlikely to benefit from a prescription of direct instruction in consonant blends. In fact it may be that too much emphasis on consonant blends or other highly specific skills has contributed to the child's learning problems.

In addition much testing and observation formerly had to do with determining "levels" at which children were performing. These levels, especially reading levels, were taken seriously. If a child was shown to have a reading level of grade 3.2, for example, that artificial designation often had far more credence than any observations the classroom teacher made about the child's ability to cope with texts of varying levels of difficulty.

Salina is a case in point. Her score on a recent standardized survey showed her to be reading at a low grade-two level. Salina has read *Charlotte's*

Web and is currently reading *Pippi Longstocking,* books typically read by third and fourth graders.

The eighties and nineties have brought with them dramatically modified views on how instruction should occur. If children's learning is to be maximized, models of instruction and models of assessment/observation must be parallel. (To entertain a mismatch between the two is running the risk of inappropriate decision making.)

Perhaps one of the most dramatic differences between former and current views has to do with the distinction between observing artifacts of learning and observing the process of learning as it happens. Typically children were given tests that left a trail of filled-in blanks, answers to comprehension questions, and so on. *How* children arrived at their responses was not a consideration. Decisions had to be made on the basis of what they left on paper. We know that many creative children had to learn that frameworks guiding instruction were far different from those guiding assessment. Most of the time, children, especially the younger ones, would comply with these differences. Occasionally a child's creativity would intervene as he forgot about the sterility of tests and test-taking behavior. Natural instincts would override expectations about normal test-taking conventions. An example:

> Terry was a creative child. His wealth of knowledge was advanced far beyond his six and a half years. He shocked the teacher, his parents, and the administrative office when he, a good reader, scored at the twenty-fifth percentile on a beginning sounds test. The first inclination was to put Terry on an intensive program of beginning sounds instruction. (The diagnostic/prescriptive tradition would dictate that any sensible professional would do exactly that.) However, much to the disgust of fellow professionals, Terry's teacher decided to engage in what they called "tinkering with a test in an unprofessional manner." Perplexed about Terry's low performance she decided to ask Terry to defend some of his responses. Two of the items follow:

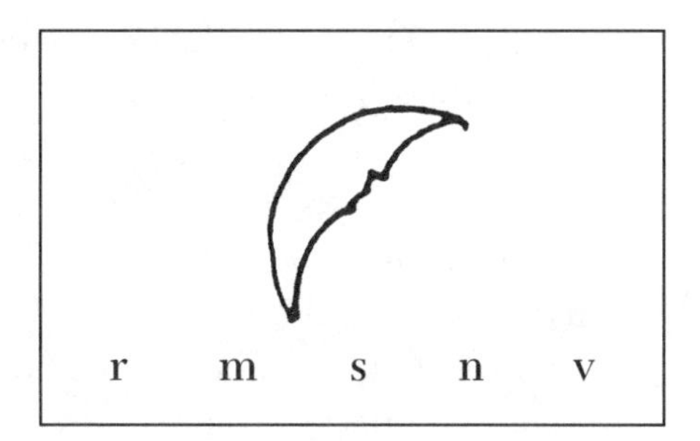

> When Terry was asked why he had circled *p* rather than the obvious *c*, Terry responded, "I knew it was a crown; I know crown starts with *c;* but I thought 'no, that's too easy; it must be *p* for *palace* because people who live in palaces wear crowns.' I knew that the next one was a moon even if it really doesn't look like a moon. I figured it had to be *night* because the moon shines at night. So I put a mark around *n* and not *m*."

The example illustrates how adults make assumptions about how children think, assumptions that are often wrong. Fortunately children aren't that predictable. The case also shows how a restrictive context for assessment limits what teachers see, even creates conditions where they are forced to see things that impede appropriate learning and instruction.

There is increasing interest in observing what children can achieve and how they go about achieving it. Feuerstein (1979), the master of dynamic assessment, holds the view that instruction is best served as we observe children in situations where they can demonstrate "peaks of performance." These situations involve providing prompts, probes, and supports that enable the child to reveal competencies that are there but that don't typically manifest themselves without support. In traditional assessment terms these were thought to be aberrations rather than windows into children's capacities. He has demonstrated that these peaks provide important hints of the capacities that generally do not manifest themselves. Traditional assessments are not designed to unearth such peaks.

Vygotsky (1978) proposed that learners operated within zones. There are certain things that they can do independently, and other things that they are able to do with the assistance of an adult or competent peer. In his view the things that a child does with the help of a peer show the capacities of the learner and allow us to see his "cutting edge of learning." The zone between what children can do independently (actual developmental level) and what they are able to accomplish with assistance (potential developmental level) Vygotsky called the zone of proximal development. Brown and Reeves (1985) referred to these zones as band widths of competence. Clay, in referring to the concept of zone, makes the following observation: "The foundation for personal success is to discover one's particular competencies. The essence of successful teaching is to know where the frontier of learning is for any pupil on a particular task" (1991: 65).

A reliable link between observation and instruction can be forged as one delves into the specific competencies, the specific zones that children traverse before our eyes and their own eyes. Such a link was not possible given the constraints of traditional assessment practices. Viewing assessment within Vygotsky's framework pushes us to the creation of strong interactive links among learning, assessment, and instruction. What is especially attractive about such a view is that it takes the focus off the blind search for the best "method" or materials for the class. A score does not dictate the child's learning future; the emphasis is child-focused. For example:

> Santu has just read, "The loud crash left the animals in a state of honour." He stops, perplexed, knowing that something is wrong. Where the teacher might just have provided the word in text, *horror*, she decided to see what strategies Santu had to figure out the word. Santu floundered when he tried to take another run at the sentence. It didn't solve the problem; it confirmed in his mind that *honour* was a wrong choice. The teacher read the first part of the sentence for him. The problem wasn't solved. The teacher asked Santu to read one more time. When Santu came to the last word, the teacher simply slipped her thumb over the "hor" of the target word, stopped for a moment, and then uncovered the remainder of the word. Santu's immediate response was *horror*. The incident confirmed to both child and teacher that Santu is monitoring for meaning and that he is quite competent to use phonic and structural cues, especially with the minor nudge from the teacher. It also revealed to the teacher that any number of "runs" on an unknown word isn't helpful if the word isn't a part of the child's vocabulary. Although Santu has spoken English for less than a year, he was able to explain from general context the meaning of the word *horror*.

A final, less subtle distinction that relates to the link between assessment and instruction has to do with what is deemed the target for change. Traditionally the learner was the target that was to be changed. Currently we are looking at how to improve the learning environment. The goal, ultimately, is to see learner change, but that will come out of rethinking and modifying instruction as we observe, and interacting with learners as they traverse their zones of proximal development (see page 61, chapter 4). Focusing on the child's learning ability is very different from trying to discover causes for learning failure within the child, which some might argue is a kind of "child focus." An example:

> One of many recent calls came from a teacher who obviously was under some pressure from parents of a child who was having difficulty. In short, Wes, a second grader, was not reading and was still engaging in "scribbles typical of three- and four-years olds." There was cause for concern. As I probed and probed about the child's responses to various instructional scenarios, all I received in

> reply was, "We have tried everything, and nothing works; Wes learns differently from other children. He sees the world differently." I kept probing till I was assured that the teacher and parents were convinced that there was something of a perceptual nature that kept the child from learning to read and write. The message was abundantly clear: let's find something within the learner that is wrong and fix it. Wes had evidently received nothing except an intelligence test (high average) and some outdated scale that involved drawing shapes from memory (which Wes related later were "dumb" and "baby stuff"). Nobody in the school could tell me anything about Wes's response to changes in instruction. In fact, nobody was really able to tell me much about him at all except that he was intelligent, well-mannered, but "just not learning."

Wes's case demonstrates how we search for learning solutions in the wrong places. Before Wes can benefit from school instruction, someone will need to find out something about his zones—the competencies he has already demonstrated—and the kinds of assistance that help him traverse within these zones. I am not implying that Wes may not have some perceptual problems—I have no way of knowing from anything I heard. Regardless, we need to find out what environmental changes will result in responsive learning. Some would say that Wes needs a battery of tests. I say that he needs close, intelligent, ongoing observation and perhaps some consultation between teacher and other professionals if learning patterns do *not* change. Right now the gaze is restricted—it is impossible for the people around Wes to observe him in the right places and thus make a positive difference. One's view about children, assessment, learning, and instruction either widens the gaze—that is, what one is able to see—or restricts and limits what one sees. The latter, unfortunately, is the case for Wes.

In traditional assessment little was said about advocacy for children. That doesn't mean that educators wilfully worked against the best interests of children. It's just that decisions were made in what today may seem cold and calculated ways. We hear more today about teachers as advocates for children; it seems to me that advocacy is much more closely linked to day-to-day observations about children.

THE CONTEXT FOR OBSERVATION

In traditional assessment we made every attempt to control the context during assessment. Every learner received the same tasks with the same set of instructions, given in the same tone of voice at the same time. This represented a supposedly controlled scientific setting that allowed us to compare what children could do under the same conditions.

The examiner/examinee relationship was assumed to be inconsequential. The roles were clearly defined—static and predictable. The examiner was in control of the agenda and the flow of information. Johnston (1992) refers to the power differential that is explicit in this kind of setting. What is most remarkable, perhaps, is that we have known for decades that for children to demonstrate their full potential as learners, they must find themselves in settings where they are comfortable. If anything, a traditional assessment setting was programmed to intimidate learners—and teachers.

One of the ironies of former assessment schemes was that children were placed in settings that were deliberately limiting in language. The language used for assessment and its administration constituted a genre all its own. Apart from the deliberate controlling tone of the language, it was a language restricted only to testing settings—and assumed to be understood by children.

Currently we try to place children in circumstances where they can demonstrate the best of their capacities and abilities. We bend over backwards to free the conditions under which we observe them rather than control them. We are not interested in making comparisons with others; we want to observe personal learning over time. We encourage children to defend their responses as it is from these statements that we frequently gain the most insight. We encourage them to ask for clarification if they don't understand. In fact *their* questions are often more informative than their responses to *our* questions.

We now recognize the tremendous impact of the social setting. The relationship between the one who observes and the learner is critical. It is not a simple matter of establishing rapport for the "occasion" in order to "soften" the client for testing. We are interested in ongoing, genuine relationships that open the door for both the learner and teacher. Friendly, trusting relationships don't suddenly turn on when it's time to learn and then turn off when it's time for assessment. In fact children who have been overtested develop a paranoia about testing; they suspect at times that they are being tested when, in fact, that is not so. This occurred with Karen, who had been working with me informally over a period of time. We were very comfortable with each other. On one occasion she was reading just to see how fluently she could manage a piece of text she had selected. She was happy to read; in fact, she was quite enthusiastic. She read with remarkable fluency—quite at odds with her past performance of plodding, word-by-word sounding and sputtering.

Karen had previously paid little attention to sentence boundaries, as meaning had been far removed from her prime motivation. While she was reading this time, I noted something of interest that I felt worthy of record, and quickly scribbled a note to myself. Karen's quick and decisive response was "I didn't know this was a test"; she then continued to read. Her "before" and "after" fluency patterns are noted below. The phrase lines below the text indicate where Karen made natural breathing, intonation, and thinking junctures.

Before interruption

The first days of the steam trains were exciting and dangerous. The trains looked like big monsters. They threw off sparks and smoke, ran off the track, and

After interruption

coast to the west. New towns sprung up in places that were once prairie. When the track was finished, people rode trains from one end of the country to the other. Trains helped our country grow.

Karen clearly had a learning/instructional register and a testing register. Her ways of responding in the two registers were dramatically different. Before she assumed I was testing her, Karen read with obvious meaning, reflected not only in her phrasing, but also in the way in which she spontaneously corrected any words that did not fit with overall meaning. After she went into her test-taking mode, her voice became strained and her reading labored and fragmented. A complete breakdown in meaning was reflected in the abandonment of self-monitoring. The few attempts at correction resulted in meaningless substitutions. Worst of all Karen felt that I had betrayed her—at least for a time.

I asked Karen to listen to her reading, which I had taped, an exercise that offered considerable insight into her perception about "good reading" and what one does in attempting to read well. I include a short portion of the conversation we had to indicate a sense of her perceptions:

Karen: *I changed my reading in line 8.*

Carl: *How did you change it?*

Karen: *I stopped being sloppy. I was real careful.*

Carl: *Were you not careful in the first part?*

Karen: *Not really. I read fast and I went back.*

Carl: *Why did you stop doing that in line 8?*

Karen: *Because I didn't know it was a test. And then I tried hard.*

Carl: *Do you try harder on a test than you do when you are just reading in class?*

Karen: *Yes!*

Carl: *Why?*

Karen: *Teachers, and... like you... put things in my report and Mom wants me to try the best.*

Carl: *When we started reading, why did you not think that was a test?*

Karen: *Well... like... we talked about it... to help me... and then you asked me some questions... just in talking... you helped me at first.*

Carl: *And then it's not a test?*

Karen: *No!* [without hesitation] *We just talked... and then I just said what I thought in reading. I wasn't really thinking hard. Also, you helped me.*

(Braun, Rennie, and Gordon 1987: 286)

Karen is able at a moment's notice to switch from an exploratory, relaxed, risk-taking stance to a careful, constrained, unnatural test-taking one. The greatest travesty is that Karen perceives herself to be doing her best reading when she is in the test-taking mode. In this mode she leaves the teacher and parent with artifacts of her learning that totally mask what she is capable of doing under natural conditions of support. It provides a "window," but it's the wrong window; any instructional inferences that are based on this information can only lead to long-term failure. Her testing behavior all but closes the door to appropriate instructional adjustment. Karen, like many others, is concerned about the consequences of test results: "What happens to me if I don't do well?" Children in these circumstances suspect the worst. These fears and suspicions create conditions that inhibit learning.

Traditionally our interest was in solo performance. Many of the richest insights in classrooms today come from observing children interacting in natural contexts. The ways in which children respond to one another, the statements they make when they ask for help from a peer, and the responses they provide when a peer asks for help reveal much about their thinking of language and language learning. Sometimes we deliberately ask children to solve a series of problems together to stimulate talk about their strategies for problem solving. An example:

> Jennie, who had been referred for special help in reading and writing, was reluctant to talk about her thinking strategies. It was difficult to determine whether she was simply reluctant to talk, whether she didn't have the language appropriate to talk about strategies, or whether she simply assumed the passive role: "You tell me what to do, and I'll comply."
>
> One day we asked Jennie to read a selection with a partner, one who was also having problems. We told them that the selection was going to be too hard for them to read individually, but thought that together they might be able to manage it. The two were left alone; we taped the session from an adjoining room.
>
> Jennie, the elder of the two (though not necessarily the better reader), immediately took charge. Among other things, she revealed that she knew exactly what to do when she came to a word she didn't know. Among her statements were: "You have to go back to see what will make sense; I think that word is *stick,* it has the same end as *sick; silly* makes sense in this part, but look at the title, the word can't be *silly,* the title then wouldn't make sense," and so on.
>
> Jenny displayed an amazing array of strategies, some of which she had been using in tutorial sessions, often only after prompting and probing. When the two children were asked to view the tape, Jenny told us that she hadn't known that she knew some of the things that she had demonstrated on the tape.

This scenario demonstrates a number of important issues relevant to current views on assessment/observation. First, if an adult is in control, the child feels no need to develop problem-solving strategies. "Someone else will help me" is the all too pervasive mind-set. In other words, there is no need to stretch (the first rule if we wish to promote wide-scale mediocrity). Second, we have long known that language is essential for learning. To talk through a problem reveals what strategies one really has available to solve it. Such a situation revealed to Jenny and her mentors some of the problem-solving secrets that lay dormant. The previous example demonstrates once again the intimate tie between assessment and learning.

In summary how we act, how we talk, even whether we *will* talk depends on the learning context. At the same time these behaviors themselves create a changing context. It *does* matter who is present, what the setting is, who is assumed to be in control, and what the perceived consequences of the encounter are. An interactive environment is just as valid for observation and assessment as it is for language learning. How we look at this aspect of assessment is likely the most dramatic departure from traditional thinking about assessment and observation of children's learning.

MULTIPLE INDICATORS OF LEARNING

Those who employed traditional assessment relied on limited "samples" of children's performance. This applied as much to tests prescribed to be administered by teachers as it did to tests administered by outside specialists. These samples often consisted of written responses to questions on short pieces of text—for the most part, contrived text. Children were expected to respond to multiple-choice questions. There was little concern that children were forced to provide "one, and only *one* correct" response. There was little concern that what they were asked to do in a testing situation did not match what they did in regular learning/instructional situations. Brown and Reeves characterize traditional views of assessment as reliance on "static snapshot descriptions of developmental status frozen in time and welded to particular task environments" (1985: 71). The corresponding analogy for current views would be of an ongoing video, discussed with the learners for elaboration and clarification.

The traditional hallmark of testing young learners was the readiness test (which still persists in certain areas). Whether or not children felt comfortable with paper-and-pencil activities was of little concern. These assessment devices sampled limited domains—letter knowledge, beginning and ending sound knowledge, word and shape discrimination, and so on. The sampling was limited to the graphophonemic area. Even within this domain, the samples did not necessarily demonstrate the child's true knowledge, and certainly did not reveal his ability to integrate and apply knowledge. These instruments had some statistical properties capable of predicting future reading achievement, at least to an extent. Predicting who will fail, however, has never been a productive exercise.

Decisions were frequently made either at the school level or by outside experts strictly on the basis of test results and without regard for the teachers' better judgment. Reading instruction was frequently withheld from children deemed not ready for reading. For children who were considered "ready," instruction was based on these limited samples. This tied children into a limited—and limiting—framework for ongoing reading growth. Today we recognize that many of these children, through inappropriate instruction, were programmed to fail. As testimony to children's abilities to find their way through mazes we create, however, many learned to read in spite of these formal reading programs.

Today we realize how important it is that children demonstrate what they are able to do along the widest possible spectrum of learning. We want observations to be grounded in classroom reality. Naturally, if we are interested in a child's reading strategies, we want to observe him reading in many contexts and for varied purposes—real reading of different types of materials. We are less concerned about correct answers than we are about the strategies children use to arrive at answers and their capacities to hypothesize why or why not an answer is reasonable. We observe the young learner in many settings not to determine "readiness"—all children are ready. We observe to determine where they are along the spectrum of reading and writing development. Through our observations—and their own—we determine where children are and then attempt to adjust learning environments to maximize their continued learning.

Skills were the essence of traditional assessment; the more specifically one was able to pinpoint skill gaps, the more comprehensive the picture of the learner was assumed to be. Reading assessment measurement was frequently based on vocabulary, word recognition, and comprehension. The frameworks that drove the search for comprehension skills (some variant of literal, interpretive, and inferential) thought to be important were taxonomies like the well-known Bloom's Taxonomy and assorted versions of it. Bloom's Taxonomy, a framework of thinking levels, is assumed to represent the range of learning of children, beginning at the lower end of the spectrum with knowledge, recall, and recognition and moving toward comprehension and application. The different levels of the taxonomy were represented in curriculum by specific goals (behavioral objectives). Test items were devised to assess student attainment of these goals. Paper-and-pencil responses to questions, which made up the bulk of the test for older children, were assumed to tap comprehension; assorted pieces of graphophonemic skills tasks plus responses to short bits of contrived text (comprehension) comprised the test environment for younger children.

Formal tests have undergone changes in the last decade and most of these changes represent improvements. The basic thinking behind their function and the underlying assumptions about their significance have not changed to any great extent, however. Even the best of them fail to derive a real picture of strategies children employ to learn reading—strategies that inform us how to modify instructional environments. Some questions that remain unanswered with formal tests are: What are the resources the child has to solve a text problem? Does the child have the strategies to determine when meaning is breaking down? What are his own perceptions of the kinds of assistance that are going to be helpful for growth in reading and writing? Do the questions she poses go beyond asking "What is this word?" or "How do you spell that word?" Is he developing strategies to help himself now and as a future learner? Are her strategies refined to the point where they are called forth automatically, or are they at the stage where they still require conscious effort along with some assistance?

Those are some of the questions asked by teachers who want children to become autonomous learners, and who are searching for ways to foster that independence. Those are questions light years removed from the questions that drove, and continue to drive, traditional forms of assessment.

OBSERVATION: A COLLABORATIVE VENTURE

Not many years ago asking children to collaborate in the assessment/observation process would have been viewed as bizarre. After all, assessment, like instruction, was the domain of the professional. In addition a kind of aura existed, a special kind of power that clearly separated the professional from the learner (teachers were not considered learners in any significant sense).

Today's view is that children must be invited into the total learning process so that the best possible decisions can be made about their learning. As mentioned, children are more likely to take ownership of their learning if they understand more about their own resources as learners. It is unreasonable to expect them to assume ownership if they are kept in the dark about the observation/assessment process. Ownership means that the learner is aware of what is going on throughout the whole process and, under able guidance, takes responsibility for his own learning. Collaboration is more than sharing secrets *about* the child *with* the child; it is about engaging the child in an ongoing search for the secrets. The foundations of control and ownership lie in the child's growing understanding of his learning.

Parents can and should be invited to share what they know about their children as learners. Children demonstrate aspects of learning at home that are not readily visible at school, and vice versa. Collaboration between parent and teacher is especially important when the child makes the transition from learning at home to learning at school. Children, during this time, form expectations about what is and what is not appropriate at school. Often they can't see how their previous home learning extends to school. Disjunction between the two worlds unfortunately lays waste to much potential. Parents can frequently help prevent learning tangles, and help sort them out when they occur.

Increasingly, teachers collaborate with other professionals in the assessment process, especially where children's learning appears to be at risk. Psychologists, for example, are no more able to work in a vacuum than are teachers. The process becomes one of sharing information with a wide range of sources—parents, teachers, psychologists, children themselves—and then putting together a tentative picture. The picture can then be observed, as adaptations are made to the child's learning environment. The process is ongoing. How does the child respond to modified learning conditions? How do these modifications change the picture over time? Are continuing collaborative observations in order? These are just a few of the questions raised.

ASSESSMENT AGENDAS, OWNERSHIP, AND POLITICS

Traditionally agenda ownership was not discussed. Any serious assessment agenda was assumed to be the exclusive domain of people outside the classroom. That doesn't mean, of course, that teachers didn't do their own content testing for end-of-term reports. But deciding when and how kids should be assessed or making a serious decision about a child's future was usually determined by those outside the teacher's domain. This external control problem has been exacerbated by public disenchantment with schools, and with concerns that schools are not addressing "the basics." While the improvement of instruction and learning is the ultimate assessment goal of provincial/state departments or district education offices, in fact the result typically is a narrowing of curriculum; that is teachers are pushed to teach what children will be tested on, often against the teacher's professional judgment. It is hard to imagine how teachers can possibly do a more effective job of teaching when demands from outsiders do not respond to directions in instruction. As long as assessment for purposes of accountability and assessment to inform and fine-tune instruction are seen as different entities, there is little hope, in my view, for substantive change. That issue is addressed in much greater depth in chapter 4.

How this political distribution of power has affected teacher morale and professionalism has only recently become a topic for discussion. It really comes down to a question of who controls the assessment agendas. Some teachers have begun the fight to gain at least a semblance of control over that agenda. Interestingly that line of thinking has come from teachers who are more reflective about their teaching and practice and more convinced of the critical need to fully integrate assessment, learning, and instruction.

Concluding Comments

In this chapter I have outlined some of the essential differences between traditional and current views of observation/assessment. I've highlighted how current views are moving towards integrating day-to-day observation with learning and instruction. These links become the driving force of what children and teachers engage in daily.

One of the most dramatic differences regarding beliefs about assessment pivots on current views related to the environment or context in which assessment takes place. In fact everything hinges on the context. Rather than control the context in a scientific way, we try to change the context in creative ways so that children can demonstrate their potential in the widest possible sense. This brings into play the teacher's creative powers as well. No longer can she rely on an instrument created by someone else; she is the instrument. Context—creating the best possible learning environment—means the freedom for both teacher and child to take risks, freedom to show what a child and teacher are capable of doing. Samples are not limited to a few snapshots that may catch the learner smiling; there are many poses—smiles, frowns, warts and all. We observe learning in as many contexts as possible. We are not concerned about sampling in the traditional sense. The samples are there as long as there are children and as long as there are teachers. There are few opportunities for significant pieces of information to fall between the cracks.

Collaboration—among professionals, parents, and with children themselves—is fundamental to assessment that informs learning and guarantees learning success. For optimum collaboration the agenda for assessment and for learning must be the undisputed domain of the person who has the greatest professional knowledge about the child—the teacher. The teacher is then free to invite other collaborators to share in the process of kid watching.

REFERENCES

Bloom, B. *Taxonomy of Educational Objectives: Handbook One, Cognitive Domain.* New York: McKay Publications, 1956.

Braun, C., B. Rennie, and C.J. Gordon. "An Examination of Contexts for Reading Assessment." *Journal of Educational Research* 80 (5): 283-289 (1987).

Brown, A., and R. A. Reeves. *Bandwidths of Competence: The Role of Supportive Contexts in Learning and Development*. Champaign Urbana (Technical Report, No. 336), University of Illinois Center for the Study of Reading, 1985.

Clay, M. M. *Becoming Literate: The Construction of Inner Control.* Portsmouth, NH: Heinemann, 1991.

Feuerstein, R. *The Dynamic Assessment of Retarded Performers.* Baltimore, MD: University Park Press, 1979.

Johnston, P. H. *Constructive Evaluation of Literate Activity.* New York: Longman, 1992.

Vygotsky, L. S. *Mind In Society: The Development of Higher Mental Processes*, edited by M. Cole et al. Cambridge, MA: Harvard University Press: 1978.

TRADITIONAL (focuses on child's skill development)	CURRENT (focuses on children and the development of strategies (i.e., child-centered))
skills-focused observation/assessment	child-focused observation
interest in comparative profiles	interest in individual learning profiles
test results show where skill deficits lay; assessment and instruction linked only incidentally, if at all; testing/observation determine "level" child is performing at— assessment results assumed to be reliable and valid guides to instructional needs	models of instruction and models of assessment/observation must be parallel and so closely linked that the questions of reliability and validity become obsolete—how a child arrives at response as important as actual response
"peaks of performance" are aberrations, not windows into children's capacities	instruction best served when children observed in situations where they can demonstrate "peaks of performances"
focus on search for best "method" or materials for class	learners operate within zones; focus on individual learner zone to suggest appropriate instruction and choice of materials
teachers monitor children	self-monitoring is an important process to be observed
testing agendas for the most part owned by external people	testing (assessment), learning, and instruction so intimately linked that the ownership of assessment resides with the children and their teachers
learner target to be changed	learning environment target to be changed
focus on child's failures	focus on child's learning abilities
attempts to control the context during assessment: learners receive same tasks, instruction, and so on. Assumption that examiner/examinee relationship inconsequential	no attempts to control but to free the context; learners are not compared, are encouraged to ask questions; understanding of the importance of the consequences of the teacher/learner relationship
main interest in "solo performance"	main interest in interaction
assessment relies mainly on tests	assessment based on observing day-to-day learning
instruction decisions and assessment often made by outside "experts"	instruction decisions often a collaborative venture with students/other professionals

Traditional Assessment: Albatross Around the Neck of Teacher Change

3

We hear much today about school reform, educational revolution, and the need to prepare children for the challenges of the year 2000. Much of this talk takes place in the absence of teachers—on the explicit assumption that they are rear-line players in this major drama. Much of the rhetoric points to the need for teachers to change. While that need may be real in some instances, the message is clearly that teachers need to *be* changed once bureaucrats have decided how this should be done. In short, teachers are seen as objects that will be changed. I suggest that education will best be served when we learn to expect teachers to become change agents (Braun 1990). I believe that many of the pivotal issues constraining teachers from assuming a dramatic role as agents of change involve firmly entrenched beliefs and attitudes about accountability and the politics of accountability.

Curriculum is either limited or enhanced by prevailing views about assessment. Teacher effectiveness is either limited or enhanced by the ways in which responsibility, authority, and control are given to the teacher. I believe that the way in which observation/assessment is viewed is the key to teacher change and development. Pressures that emanate from public and administrative notions about assessment often inhibit teachers—to the point where they view change as negative. That may sound pessimistic; however, we *can* transform these prevailing views. But first we need to come to terms with the strong influence that assessment has on learning and instruction, and ultimately, on teacher and school change. In this chapter I present a detailed discussion of the serious pitfalls of traditional assessment practices set against the rhetoric of change that accompanies many current discussions about assessment.

Accountability and Teacher Authority and Control

"He who pays the fiddler names the tune" is an apt metaphor for the public control over what happens in a child's education. That is neither good nor bad. Views about what the tune should be and the methods used to assess whether the tune has been learned or not often lead to disturbing consequences, however. In the last two decades accountability pressures have taken their toll on teacher creativity and initiative. Public and political views often push teachers into corners where assessment for accountability and assessment to fine-tune instruction run counter to each other. In other words accountability pressures generally run counter to effective instructional and learning practices. The discussion of traditional versus child-focused perspectives in chapter 2 supports this view.

BUREAUCRATIC LAYERS OF CONTROL

Frequently the drama of control results in schisms not only between teachers and the public, but also between teachers and administrators (and sometimes among administrators at various levels of the bureaucracy) who see themselves on the front line of defense.

For example Uplands Elementary School has just survived, though barely, the annual large-scale assessment of its language arts program. The kids there have not done as well as kids in the rest of the city, even the rest of the province. The superintendent's office has held meetings with administrators and consultants. The results of these meetings have been made public:

- Schools with lower than average test scores "will come to grips with solid teaching in the basic skills."
- Teachers, especially those in the lower grades, will devote more time to direct instruction, and less time "doing centers and freewheeling activities."
- Teachers will provide building principles with both long-term and short-term instructional plans.

➤ Regular system-wide formal assessments are mandated to ensure that instructional objectives are achieved.

Mr. Small, the principal, has just called a staff meeting to "lower the boom." After all, low scores reflect poorly not only on teachers, but also on administrators. Let's eavesdrop for a few minutes to see what Mr. Small is going to lay on the already fragile egos of the school's teachers:

Mr. Small: *It is no secret that our children have not performed well on the last round of tests. I would say that the performance is disgraceful. I had everything short of a pledge from most of you that your "new approaches" would work better than what we have been doing in the past. What have I got for it?* [Dead silence.] *This will not be a long meeting. I have four mandates from the superintendent's office, and I will simply read them to you. I will not mince words. Your own evaluations will be based on your commitment to these mandates.*

Ms. Stein: *You realize, Mr. Small, that some of the approaches some of us have been trying have created a lot of enthusiasm for learning, and we know that children have benefited immeasurably as a result.*

Mr. Small: *Your choice of words, Ms. Stein, is strange. Obviously, the benefits have not been "measurable." You know the rules. We have mandates; our job is to live with the mandates. Quite clear!*

Mr. Thom: *There have been kids in my class who used to have serious problems with both their reading and writing. I have seen remarkable growth; somehow the tests we used just didn't show what the kids had learned.*

Mr. Small: *I announced at the outset that this was going to be a short meeting. Some of you seem to misunderstand; we are not here to negotiate. We have mandates, and that's that!*

The above represents a worst-case scenario of teachers versus the test. And teachers in this kind of circumstance, especially if they are untenured, don't stand a chance. Often, they are forced to do a job that fails to meet their own expectations. At best, they are forced to engage in instructional practices that are in clear violation of administrative edicts.

Nancy Larrick recounts a similar experience in an inner-city school:

> P.S.192, on New York's West Side, had been listed as one of the worst schools in the state. It had more immigrants than any other school in the New York area. Ninety-two percent of the children came from homes below the poverty level. Eighty-six percent of the children spoke no English when they entered school.
>
> The goal of the kindergarten program in this particular school was to "offer children the opportunity to learn to read successfully in an unpressured, pleasurable environment" (1989: 1). Everything that teachers did was geared to that end. By the end of the year, all 255 children were able to read their dictated stories and the simple books that they had been exposed to. Some were, in the teachers' estimation, reading at a grade-two level. Best of all, they loved to read stories and were proud to be readers.
>
> The program persisted through first grade with equal success. Children were enthusiastic about reading and writing and they felt good about their accomplishments. But the next year, they faced the phonics-based reading test mandated for all second graders in New York City. These children, who were reading "on grade" or higher, made a poor showing on the test. Although they could read far beyond expectations for children in that area, they fell apart when asked to mark long and short vowels in a list of words read to them by the test administrator. As a result, over the loud protests of the teachers, principal, and parents, the incoming district superintendent eliminated the program. Now, Larrick says, "All kindergarten and first-grade children are spending an hour and a half each day on phonics, with a series workbook."

These two vignettes show the power of bureaucracy, power that is blind not only to the needs of children but also to the needs of teachers. In the first instance the principal is pushed to a position by central office, though in this case it was never clear whether or not he had been party to the decision. Regardless, he did not resist the mandate to change instruction. In the second instance power and control appear to reside in one person. The superintendent answers what he interprets to be the demand for accountability from the larger public, ignoring the pleas not only of local administrators but also of the parents. This perception of accountability often brings the wheels of change to a grinding halt. That certainly was the case in P.S.192.

What accounts for the apparent resistance to change in education and more particularly to change in instruction of reading and writing? Why is it that despite dramatic evidence of effective learning, the politics of education insist that teachers use assessment practices from another era?

BELIEFS IN THE MYSTICAL POWERS OF TESTS

I believe that actions like those seen in the previous two examples show a complete lack of understanding of how unilateral edicts and mandates affect the dignity of teachers and ultimately the lives of children. The message to teachers is that their judgment means less than the marks children make on paper—that in spite of their day-to-day observation of children, when decisions are being made, their judgment doesn't amount to anything. The teachers in P.S. 192 knew that their children were reading. More important, they knew that the children *liked* reading, by far the best guarantee of success, the best defense against long-term failure. They knew the children read well without knowing anything about long and short vowels. (No doubt, many of these same teachers learned about long and short vowels only as they started to work with commercial "instructional" materials.)

Beliefs in the objectivity of traditional tests as opposed to the selective subjectivity of teachers account for much of the continuing reliance on "scientific" test instruments. Further, the documentation in testing manuals about reliability and validity has a scientific ring to it. Such pseudo-scientific claims about the properties of tests dupe many into believing in their practical significance—and continue to keep test publishers in business. That the children in P.S. 192 were judged on an instrument that didn't even measure reading seems never to have been questioned. Gross mismatches between test purpose and curriculum are typically ignored by those who prefer to trust "science" rather than sound practical judgment. I recall a telephone call from a superintendent involved in the case of a child whose parents were threatening serious action:

> Having moved from another province, documentation in hand, Steve confused and frustrated the people in his new school. His file proved to be a maze of conflicting test data. From his previous school he had an overall reading score of grade 3.7, a comprehension score of 2.9, and a word analysis score of 4.8. He was given a series of tests shortly after his arrival at his new school, a response to parental demand. His new profile looked vastly different: composite reading score, grade 1.9; comprehension, grade 1.6; word study, 2.4.
>
> Steve's parents were understandably confused and upset. His father asked, "How could Steve have regressed in such a short time?" They were not about to take his failure passively. After many meetings with the teacher, resource teacher, and psychologist, they took their threats directly to the superintendent's office. The irony of it, the superintendent's call to me, was a plea for an

> explanation: how was it possible to get such discrepancies on tests that were "reliable and valid"? Even more ironic, he expected the resource teachers were simply incompetent to "handle testing."

The case illustrates how test-score talk reigns over common sense when the heat is on. It also underlines the distrust in teachers' abilities even to manage a test. The resistance to change generated by public pressure, then, is motivated partly by firmly ingrained beliefs about the mystical powers of commercially packaged tests. These "instruments" are shrouded in a jargon of promises about their potential to tell the public and the administration with precision "where children are"—especially in relation to children in other schools and school jurisdictions. That these instruments tell blatant lies about children's learning, or at the very least, distort the truth about what they have learned (and what teachers have taught) is rarely considered. And when teachers do raise the argument, it is looked upon as professional self-defense against poor teaching. The validity of the objections is swept under the carpet.

It's a sad comment that teachers have often been led to doubt their own observations about children. Imagine what happens to curriculum and instruction in settings where accountability under pressure is tantamount. Planned, substantive, long-term change is unlikely to occur under such circumstances.

The curriculum shrinkage that ensues from this pressure seems to matter little except to teachers. They continue to be pushed to prove in quantifiable terms that learning has taken place. To put it bluntly, teachers are pressured to use the machinery from the forties and fifties to help children face the learning demands of the nineties. "Literacy is seen as a commodity" (Neilsen 1986) that can be measured the way we measure concrete reinforcements and shoe sizes. Our general preoccupation with measurement and our penchant for applying industrial models to explain and rationalize learning problems fit completely with public demands for accountability. That these models represent a complete and utter misfit with current views about children's learning and the creation of effective instructional environments is irrelevant. The resulting tension leaves teachers and children in a quandary; it is antithetical to substantive change. The persistent disregard for teachers' professional judgment is likely the most pervasive obstacle to teacher change —and to educational change. It all but guarantees loss of vigor and energy to push teachers to new personal and professional frontiers. It challenges any move to take risks—after all why bother? This disregard obliges teachers to maintain the status quo; to take the line of least resistance. An environment for children where creative learning is far removed from the instructional agenda is the result.

PUBLIC TEST-SCORE HUNGER

Closely linked to the perception about the mystical powers of tests, we have, as Mayher and Brause (1986) have stated, made the public test-score hungry. Teachers often become weary when after arduous attempts to document improvements in children's learning in the most creative ways, the parent waits for the first wedge of silence to inquire, "But where is my child *really* at? What was his score on the test that was given last week?" The all-too-typical scenario follows:

> Derek, a nine-year-old, has had problems learning to read. These problems surfaced in his first year of school when the teacher reported to the parents that Derek had difficulty "attending to tasks, learning his ABCs, remembering words, learning sounds, and doing numbers." At the end of the year Derek was given a battery of tests that confirmed everything the teacher had reported. The parents seemed willing to accept this "confirmation" of the teacher's assessment of Derek. Derek struggled for the next two years making limited progress, becoming increasingly bored and distracted, and generally, socially marginalized.
>
> In fourth grade Derek was assigned a new teacher who was not satisfied with his demonstrations of "helplessness" and his complete lack of engagement in either individual or group learning activities. She met with Derek and his parents early in the school year to get a more comprehensive picture of this young learner who puzzled her to the point of distraction. The teacher showed the parents a sampling of Derek's work that demonstrated some glimmers of hope. This progress was the result of some of the strategies she and Derek had initiated. The parents were unable to come up with one positive statement about Derek's accomplishments either at home or at school. They seemed uninterested in any of the teacher's talk about Derek's improvement (a demonstration of "diagnostic solace"). They were comfortable with the knowledge that Derek had a "learning disability."
>
> Needless to say, Derek's teacher was discouraged. However, on the strength of the minuscule bits of evidence of learning she was able to see, she persisted. Gradually, through cooperative project work, much individual and group conference work, Derek started to become involved. To both the teacher's and

> Derek's amazement, the young learner made massive strides. The teacher documented every evidence of learning—journal entries, recordings of his reading, and especially Derek's own notes about his learning.
>
> In mid-November, jubilant about the prospect of reporting success, Derek's teacher invited the parents for a conference. She and Derek presented the parents with the most elaborate display of Derek's accomplishments. The parents seemed pleased, though they did not ask a single question during the conference. Three questions, however, at the end of the conference were revealing: "What is his reading level?" "Does this mean that Derek is no longer a learning disability?" "Are you going to get him tested?"

This display, which combined the teacher's and Derek's own records with relevant samples of his work, provided impressive evidence of his accomplishments. However, it was less important than the "evidence" his parents thought resided in externally constructed tests. Unfortunately, their attitude is not uncommon. It represents a pervasive dilemma. The pressures created by test-score hunger will persist until we are able to counteract the pressure with convincing evidence that testing, and especially large-scale testing of children, creates more problems than it solves. Creative solutions will continue as more and more teachers and administrators see the power that resides in an integrated triad of assessment, learning, and instruction. The benefits will have to be publicly and convincingly demonstrated, not only by individual teachers, but by teachers *with* administrative support.

THE "GOOD OLD DAYS" PHENOMENON

Prevailing views on accountability reside in the beliefs and memories of parents, and their own childhood learning experiences (most viewed through rose-tinted glasses). I am often surprised by the allegiance of parents to the way in which they think they were taught. "It worked well for me" is a common retort to the suggestion that Johnny might benefit from instruction that differs dramatically from that his parent received. Even the most perfunctory discussion frequently discloses that, in spite of their perceived success as readers, many parents don't read. They often admit that they have never really enjoyed reading or writing. Again, I must document this very important issue with a real-life demonstration:

> My daughter Winnifred, a young, bright-eyed, enthusiastic teacher, was prepared to change the world, certainly the world of young children's learning.

> And she did change the world of some of her first graders—in significant ways. They loved to read, they loved to write, they scripted reader's theater pieces, performed their pieces, and so on. Things were going well—or so she thought.
>
> Some parents started asking questions:"Why don't you use a set of readers in your class?" "Why don't children finish some of their stories?" By February, these parents had generated group pressure. They circulated a community questionnaire, then consulted with a school board member. Serious business—despite the fact that children were learning and *enjoying* learning. In conversation, parents revealed that they felt disoriented and insecure with a program that was so different from their own experiences, or the memories of these experiences (Braun 1987).

This script has been played out in many parts of the country over the past ten years. It demonstrates an inertia that places pressure on teachers by undermining their authority and stripping them of control over teaching and learning agendas. Unchecked, it becomes a serious threat to educational/teacher change. The solution to this problem is discussed in chapter 4 (see page 67), and provides considerable hope for long-term teacher change and improved learning environments for children. This is true especially in circumstances where the administrator understands curriculum and believes in teachers.

ACCOUNTABILITY DEMANDS AND TEACHER PRACTICE

The public fails to understand the potential negative social and academic consequences resulting from unwarranted accountability demands. I have alluded earlier to constraints placed on teacher practice by these demands, but the problem is sufficiently critical to examine in more detail. Madaus makes the point that once "technologies" (streamlined systems of testing, scoring, and reporting) become established, they take on a life of their own. Once the testing process is in motion, it "proceeds on its own momentum irrespective of the intentions of the originators" (1991: 227). The most blatant corrupting consequence is that tests reduce opportunities to teach and to learn, certainly in any creative sense. Herman and Golan (1992) support the view that testing drives teachers to cover test objectives in their teaching. They often consult prior tests to assure a good match between what they teach and what they anticipate on tests. Further, teachers are pushed to spend student time on test-preparation activities, including instructions on how to take tests and worksheets that review test contents. Because tests have the power to influence what students value in education, the test preparation behavior modeled by the teacher is assumed by the students—at the expense of real learning (Madaus 1991).

Darling-Hammond makes a cogent statement about the consequences of testing:

> These instruments were initially created to make tracking and sorting of students more efficient; they are not intended to support or enhance instruction. Because of the way tests are constructed, they ignore a great many kinds of knowledge and types of performance that we expect from students, and they place test-takers in a passive role, rather than engage their capacities to structure tasks, generate ideas, and solve problems. Even the criterion-referenced tests developed in some states tend to be poor measures of curriculum attainment and of students' abilities to undertake independent tasks.... Many tests now being used fail to measure students' higher-order cognitive abilities or to support their capacities to perform real-world tasks (1991: 220-221).

Lieberman points out that tests have a particularly negative impact on the curriculum of less successful students. These students, she claims, receive a disproportionate share of meaningless, dull instruction. "Rarely are low-achieving students given opportunities to talk about what they know, to read books, to write, or to identify and solve real-life problems" (1991: 219). Herman and Golan (1992), in a comprehensive report documenting the negative effects of tests on teachers and learning, claim that schools serving economically disadvantaged students show more negative instructional effects than schools serving students from high- and middle-income backgrounds. That is, teachers tend to use materials with tightly controlled vocabularies, devote a great deal of time to instruction and drill of isolated skills, and generally resort to commercial worksheet activities. Teachers in these schools gave much greater attention to test content in their planning and instruction. Madaus provides an excellent "catalogue of disadvantages" of tests in his article, "The Effects of Important Tests on Students" (1991: 229).

Clearly what we believe about tests and how we act on these beliefs have important implications for learning and for the preparation of our children for life in the twenty-first century.

A comment from the aging professor in Douglas Adams' book *Dirk Gently's Holistic Detection Agency* is particularly appropriate when reflecting on the impact of testing on programs for children. The Professor of Chronology is dining with a former student at a Coleridge anniversary banquet. The professor, by his own admission, has a memory that can be compared to the Queen Alexandra Birdwing Butterfly—it is colorful, flits hither and thither, and is now, alas, almost completely extinct. As he shares some of his past with the student, he interrupts the discourse with:

> "Your past has murkier things in it than I dreamed possible, a quality, I might add, it shares with this soup." He wiped his mouth with his napkin very carefully. "I must go and have a word with the kitchen staff one day. I would like to be sure that they are keeping the right bits and throwing the wrong bits away" (p. 20).

Many well-intentioned testing schemes result in programs where the wrong bits have been kept, and the right bits thrown out. I believe that, so far, accountability pressures have resulted in instruction based on the wrong bits, often against the better judgment of teachers.

INCONGRUENT BELIEFS ABOUT ASSESSMENT AND INSTRUCTION

Many prevailing views on assessment are based on mechanistic views of the learning process; that is, knowledge can be broken down into discrete measurable pieces. Shepard, on the basis of a qualitative analysis of interview data from a "representative" sample of fifty district testing directors, found that approximately half of them operate from implicit learning theories that encourage close alignment of tests with the curriculum and "judicious teaching of tested content" (1991: 9). He found further that these beliefs derived from behaviorist theory that promotes sequential mastery of skills and behaviorally explicit testing of each learning step where items are keyed to highly specific learning objectives. For example if the objective is for the learner to be able to spell words containing "ei" and "ie" combinations, the test item will ask children to spell words with their combinations or to recognize correct spelling. Shepard notes that "the sequential, facts-before-thinking model of learning is contradicted by a substantial body of evidence from cognitive psychology" (Ibid.). Such beliefs certainly run counter to those of proponents of child-centered, whole-language instruction. Clearly there is continuing tension between paradigms that drive assessment and those that free teachers and children to risk creating optimum learning environments. These unresolved tensions stand in the way of wide-scale teacher change and overall educational reform.

Closely linked to the conflict in paradigms is the preoccupation of educators to be recognized as academics by the public (a public that includes their academic peers). We are part of the problem, having "deluded ourselves with the false hope that the public will respect us more if we learn to behave like real scientists" (Braun 1987). And this continues to result in a lot of pseudoscientific flurry couched in the jargon of "real professionals." A large part of the flurry rests in our attempts to objectify and measure, and then to dignify what we find with the "impenetrable language that passes for expertise" (Ferguson 1982). Perhaps this preoccupation is even more prevalent in the area of special education and learning disabilities than it is in the general educational realm. There is, however, hope. Poplin, a former editor of the *Learning Disabilities Quarterly*, has boldly stated that our preoccupation with objectivity has clouded much of the work with disabled persons: "Objectivity is a slippery concept in any field, but attempts at discovering objective criteria for verifying human problems is a convenient illusion behind which we can hide our incompetence in instruction" (1984: 132).

Finally, the role of assessment has implications for the prevention of learning problems. In the ideal world, assessment serves both accountability and instructional agendas. In the real world of children and teachers, the two are in opposition. Certainly current assessment trends that respond to accountability demands threaten the kind of instruction that many would like to see.

The whole accountability movement has created conditions in which teacher professionalism is compromised. Apart from the effects on curriculum and instruction, it creates tensions and competition among school personnel. Teachers feel that "pressures on principals get passed down the line" to them (Smith 1991: 9). It even creates suspicion when scores are consistently too high as this may have been the result of too much "teaching to the test." This is not unreasonable, especially for a non-tenured teacher—job survival becomes at least as important as teaching children. The emotional impact has been documented particularly among teachers of young children (Smith 1991). Guilt and anxiety are common among teachers who recognize their own instructional response to the tests, as well as among children. As one teacher pointed out: "The Iowa [standardized test] is cruel and unusual punishment." Some of the comments of teachers recorded by Smith are noteworthy: "...multiple choice testing leads to multiple choice teaching," "the methods that teachers have in their arsenal become reduced..." and "teaching becomes more test-like" (Ibid.). These kinds of feelings create tensions that maintain the status quo—and prevent teachers from risking new practices.

ACCOUNTABILITY AND CAUSAL ATTRIBUTION

Johnston makes one further point that pertains to the effects of testing—undue accountability pressures on teachers. If a teacher, for instance, finds that a particular student has a learning problem, the teacher will typically set out to discover what is at the root of the problem and try to solve the problem with the student. The solution will depend, says Johnston, on the way accountability is handled. He notes that the greater the accountability pressure, the less likely the teacher will "locate the problem in his instruction, or the administrator...[will] locate the problem in the organization of the school" (1992: 224). The goal changes from one of problem solving to one of self-defense. This shift changes the whole instructional milieu. Johnston notes that there are many ways in which students can be seen as the source of the problem:

> They can be seen as not very bright, learning disabled, unready, lazy, unmotivated. Some of the presumed causes, like dyslexia, carry a connotation of permanence but also a connotation of control... Each of these sets of attributions invokes different instructional strategies. The causal assumptions we make have serious consequences. For the sake of children, it is very important that teachers keep an open mind on this matter, and that schools are organized so that teachers can afford to seek the problem in their own practice (Ibid.).

This shift in focus, from searching one's own resources for problem-solving strategies to one of defense and blame, is the most debilitating consequence of undue, unreasoned accountability pressures. It all but justifies teachers' retreat into learned helplessness. After all, the attribution for failure resides somewhere in the brain of the child: teachers can do little to change that brain. And who would expect them to?

Stockpiling Assessment Findings: Professionals Play Doctor

The strong diagnostic/prescriptive approach of the sixties is hard to counteract. The notion that professionals could diagnose and prescribe had wide appeal in its superficial logic; it appeared as though we were able to discover the roots of a problem. Surely then we could set out in systematic fashion to cure the problem. The prescription was there, usually laid out in neat lists of strengths and weaknesses. Equally appealing was the appearance that assessment that informed instruction conveniently served accountability purposes. If the prescriptive instruction didn't take, something was probably wrong with the mind of the learner. Students for whom the prescription didn't take over a period of time were labeled learning disabled, and in the extreme, dyslexic. The solace of the label was good for the teacher/psychologist; it was even good for many parents. I am reminded of Richard Peck's statement—one of irony mixed with more truth than many would care to admit. He describes the parent of the newborn child who prays, "Lord, if he can't be gifted, make him dyslexic." I am not implying that teachers, clinicians, and other professionals did not do the best they could. But questioning test results often based on the most discrepant and obscure sources was the exception rather than the rule. That instructional environments might, in fact, be contributing to learning difficulties rather than enhancing learning was seldom if ever recognized. "Dyspedagogia," not dyslexia, may be at the root of much current adult illiteracy. The point I want to make is that when people believe in the infallibility of test results, there is little incentive for *teachers* to change—after all, there is something wrong with the *child*. In the meantime, teachers lose the incentive and inclination to "see and hear" what is really there; children are labeled, categorized, and sorted in the most bizarre ways, placed in learning environments that all but guarantee they won't learn. Many lose all vestiges of faith in themselves as learners, some as sound social beings. The cycle maintains itself. Worst of all, teachers can no longer perform one of their most critical roles—advocates for children.

To illustrate the point, I offer a thumbnail case sketch, not from the sixties, but from 1992. I like to think that this represents a blatant exception. I'm not sure about that.

> Stanley, an eleven-year-old, has exhibited learning problems ever since he started school. He has never learned to read fluently, his writing has always been "behind that of many of his peers," and his math skills have been lagging. Stanley has had bits of "special help" ever since he was in second grade, mostly on a pull-out basis, though for one full year he resided in a special class. After that he was retained. In the meantime Stanley has lost all faith in himself as a learner. More fortunate than many who have "done the circuit," he has managed to maintain some social status because of his prowess in athletics. As far as his learning is concerned, he has assumed a role of complete helplessness.
>
> Recently Stanley was given a battery of tests, the WISC-R (a commonly used intelligence test), and a standardized reading test consisting of comprehension,

> word study skills, and vocabulary. The result was a profile of his abilities, mostly deficits. His "verbal abilities" range from low average to deficient; his "non-verbal abilities" in the superior range. His overall IQ is low. Stanley's teacher and mother received the profile of the combined tests—intelligence and reading (the apples and oranges metaphor applies in the most bizarre sense). The prescription is summer school and a choice for the coming year of half-time or full-time assignment to a learning disabilities class. In the meantime, absolutely no information has been provided about the kinds of strategies that Stanley does or doesn't use, no sense of what has gone on in the classroom, no information that could ever be used by anyone to move into intelligent instruction. The decision-making route has gone directly past the teacher—from psychologist and learning assistance teacher to the parent (although with the teacher's knowledge).
>
> I asked Stanley's mother her opinion of Stanley's vocabulary level (that was his lowest score on the WISC-R). Since she has been a teacher, she has good sense about children's abilities at this age. She had always thought that his language development, including his vocabulary, was average. However, she accepted the score on this test, which she didn't understand, because it had been given by a person who "should know." When I told her the nature of the WISC-R test, however, she immediately responded, "Well, I can see where Stanley wouldn't even try on that kind of thing, especially with a stranger."

The Stanley saga is a classic case of reliance on the diagnostic/prescriptive tradition. The one ingredient missing is specific prescriptive instruction. The prescription is very general—more instruction in a learning disabilities setting. In the meantime, people around him (including his mother) keep on "playing doctor," believing that the ills in education can be cured using models that, for the most part, have been abandoned even by the medical community.

Beliefs About Assessment and Learning Environments

There is a close link between blind belief of what tests are able to do and the kinds of learning environments created for children. As mentioned earlier, low test scores have been used to validate low achievement. Further, in spite of decades of research documenting the corrupting consequences of grouping and streaming children, the practice continues in many places. We know only too well the close tie between the social grouping of the child and the kind of treatment he receives from teachers as well as other children (Allington 1983; Braun 1976, 1985; Cairney 1987). Much of the information that forms the basis for these groupings comes from inappropriate assessment sources. Once the groupings are in place, the kinds of instruction and materials these children are exposed to "confirm" that the decisions were "right."

The cycle, once in motion, tends to perpetuate itself. First, teachers tend to interrupt children assumed to have low ability two to five times more than children of higher ability (Allington 1980), regardless of the "mistake," and give these children less time to reflect on "mistakes" before providing the correct response (Pflaum, Pascarella, Boskwich, and Awer 1980). Second, children in low groups are typically given more restrictive instruction, often confined to the graphophonemic area (Allington 1980); are frequently given material at the frustration level of difficulty (Gambrell, Wilson, and Gantt 1981); and are provided with less material of literary quality (Cairney 1987). Perhaps the most deleterious consequence is that "low ability" children learn to think of themselves as stupid. In fact they attribute their lack of success to lack of ability, set low expectations for themselves, and generally, learn to live with these feelings of helplessness. In addition, as a consequence of the "academic class system," they lack stimulation (Ibid.).

The belief in tests and test scores is not the only factor that perpetuates the social classes in classrooms. Frequently beliefs about tests and beliefs about the "logic" of lowered expectations for children with low test scores come in the same package. Why would teachers change these beliefs when they see their lowered expectations confirmed by low performances from children who, in reality, have given up?

Concluding Comments

Susan Harmon gives an excellent summary of the consequences of accountability measures, especially those carried to extremes:

> What is dangerous about these demands for improvement—at best—is their stunning ignorance of methodology of how to get there [improvement of schools and learning]. Many of us know how to improve schools, and it's not by tests and mandates. Telling teachers what to teach is just as stultifying as telling

> children how to learn. Instead, like all teaching, it's slow, careful, personalized work. At their worst these reformers have backed schools, teachers, and parents into a corner, and the standards and tests have themselves become political, pedagogical, and emotional barriers to good education (1991: 16).

School change, teacher change, cannot come about as long as teachers have major positions of responsibility but have no authority. When the mystique surrounding test instruments and blind beliefs about the power of these instruments overrule what teachers see, hear, and believe, frustration and bewilderment leave their mark even on the strongest. When substantive decision making is based more on test scores and profiles than on teacher expertise and judgment, there is little incentive for teachers to change. Nor is there reason for them to continue to fine-tune their own observational strategies—a key source of professional learning.

Part of the problem is the mass confusion over the ownership of assessment agendas. Instruction is clearly the domain of the teacher. Assessment appears to have been appropriated by the "system," and worse still, by ministries of education. As a consequence teachers have been left with the responsibility for instruction but deprived of authority and control over assessment agendas. In such circumstances power differentials surface at every possible level—between teachers and school-level administrators, teachers and other professionals, such as psychologists and resource teachers, school-level administrators, and system-level administrators. That competitive, even threatening climate that develops often hampers open communication between teachers and children as well as teachers and other stakeholder professionals. Assessment, rather than serving as a potential route to informed communication among professionals, often ends in a mere stockpiling of test results along with odd unrelated bits of informal anecdotal information. These power differentials lead to suspicion, and ultimately to a posture of self-defense. Often teachers respond by searching for causes of learning failure within the child rather than in the instructional realm—resulting in a widening of the chasm between assessment and learning/instruction.

Both how children are grouped for instruction and how they are taught have a basis in beliefs about tests. Sadly not only is children's learning at stake, but so is their thinking about themselves as socially worthwhile beings.

Undue accountability pressures, then, challenge teacher control of and authority over belief and practice. And in the long term, these pressures threaten the capacity of teachers to define themselves as true professionals.

Bureaucratic functionaries cannot be expected to become agents of change. Instead they become defenseless victims of political bandwagons and slogans designed by others in the bureaucracy to keep the public wolves from their own doors. It isn't only the teachers who are the victims of long-term irresponsible political control; the ultimate price is on the heads of children whose potential as learners is at stake. In the end, all of society loses.

REFERENCES

Allington, R. "Teacher Interruption Behaviors Across Ability Groups." *Journal of Educational Psychology* 72 (1980).

———. "The Reading Instruction Provided Readers of Different Abilities." *Elementary School Journal* 83 No. 4 (1983).

Adams, D. *Dirk Gently's Holistic Detection Agency*. Toronto: Stoddart, 1987.

Braun, C. "Teacher Expectations: Socio-Psychological Dynamics." *Review of Educational Research* 4 No. 2 (Summer, 1976).

———. "Teacher Expectations and Instruction." *International Encyclopedia of Education*. (5008-5016) London: Pergamon Press, 1985.

———. "The Disabled Reader: Challenge for Change." University of Calgary Distinguished Lecture Series. University of Calgary, October, 1987.

———. Teacher Change and the Politics of Change. Speech presented at the Conference of the Alberta District Council of the International Reading Association, 1990.

Cairney, T. "The Social Foundations of Literacy." *Australian Journal of Reading* 10 (2): 84-96 (June, 1987).

Darling-Hammond, L. "The Implications of Testing Policy for Quality and Equality." *Phi Delta Kappan* 73 (3): 220-225 (1991).

Ferguson, M. *The Aquarian Conspiracy: Personal and Social Transformation in the 80's*. Los Angeles: T. J. Tarcher, 1982.

Gambrell, L. B., R. M. Wilson, and W. N. Gantt. "An Analysis of Task Attending Behaviors of Good and Poor Readers." In *Diagnostic and Remedial Reading*, edited by R. M. Wilson. Columbus, OH: C. E. Merrill, 1981.

Harmon, S. "Testing Limits." *Basic Education* 16 No. 1 (February, 1991): 1.

Herman, J., and S. Golan. *The Effects of Standardized Testing on Teachers and Learning: Another Look.* Report of National Center for Research on Evaluation, Standards, and Student Testing, Graduate School, University of Southern California at Los Angeles, 1992.

Johnston, P.H. *Constructive Evaluation of Literate Activity*. New York: Longman, 1992.

Larrick, N. "To Ride a Butterfly." *Reading in Virginia* XIV (Spring, 1989): 1-4.

Lieberman, A. "Accountability As A Reform Strategy." *Phi Delta Kappan* 73 (3): 219 (1991).

Madaus, G.F. "The Effects of Important Tests On Students: Implications for a National Examination System." *Phi Delta Kappan* 73 (3): 226-229 (1991).

Mayher, J.S., and R.S. Brause. "Learning through Teaching: Is Testing Crippling Integrated Language Education?" *Language Arts* 63 (4): 390-396 (1986).

Neilsen, L. "A Teacher's Joy: The Schooling of a Writer." Paper presented to the Fourth International Conference on the Teaching of English. Ottawa, ON, 1986.

Pflaum, S., E. Pascarella, W. Boskwich, and C. Awer. "The Influence of Pupil Behaviors and Pupil Status Factors on Teacher Behaviors During Oral Lessons Reading." *Journal of Education Research* 74: (1980).

Poplin, M. "Summary Rationalizations, Apologies and Farewell: What We Don't Know About the Learning Disabled." *Learning Disabilities Quarterly* 7 (4) (1984).

Shepard, L.A. "Psychometric Beliefs About Learning." *Educational Researcher* 20 (7): 2-16 (October, 1991).

Smith, M. L. "Put to the Test: The Effects of External Tests on Teachers." *Educational Researcher* 20 (5): 8-11 (1991).

Assessment Options: Wind Beneath the Wings of Teacher Change

4

The doom and gloom that pervades chapter 3 is not intended to discourage teachers in their roles as professionals. Rather the intent is to clarify some of the problems surrounding assessment and place them in a historical context. Hopefully this clarification will help us understand a little more fully the parameters of the "battles" so that we can deal with them more effectively. The previous chapter also underlines a critical concern—the way assessment is perceived and practiced makes all the difference in the world as to whether or not teachers become professional learners or bureaucratic functionaries.

In this chapter I play a more upbeat tune. There are, in fact, many positive moves being made in assessment in classrooms all over this continent and around the world. Unfortunately these represent islands of change—in many instances, rather isolated islands. To move from islands of change to large land masses of change, we have to show first, how assessment agendas can and should be used in the most positive ways to bring about teacher change and school change and second, how this can be done. I believe that change in thinking about assessment and assessment agendas can have significant implications for positive change.

The Classroom as Research Station

In the last ten years we have seen shifts in ways of thinking about what counts as legitimate research. What teachers do in classrooms has in many parts achieved credibility as legitimate research. The foundations of this research lie in teacher observation and the continual refinement of that observation. The classroom setting exemplifies the ideal as we attempt to test hypotheses about learning and instruction and, perhaps even more important, to generate new hypotheses about children and learning. Relationships are ready-made; no need to establish rapport to give the kids a chance. The rapport is there as a result of the teaching and learning that happens daily. The teacher reflects on her own research and that of her collaborators. It is a learning environment as much for teachers as it is for children. The lab, the research station, is where it should be—in the natural habitat of children and teachers.

There are a number of healthy spinoffs from this broadened perspective of research. First, more and more teachers see the need for support groups who share information. The members of the support group talk about their research and about learning that has taken place. Second, the networks that form become professionally supportive. They result in a kind of optimism, a feeling of hope that "what I'm doing is significant"—a feeling that change can and should come from within. No longer does the teacher view herself as an object for an external agent to change, to mold in someone else's image; she *is* the change agent. These feelings lay the foundation for self-determination and the underlying confidence to look for change in oneself. These are the feelings that will eventually change education as teachers begin to see themselves as educators in the larger sense. An example should help to underline the notion:

> Jean Whitmore has taught for fifteen years. For many years she has thought of herself as a "very traditional teacher." She says, "I was quite happy to follow the dictates of my superiors after my first two or three years in the profession. I learned to believe that as long as I followed the curriculum to my principal's satisfaction, I was a good teacher. I was never really unhappy; never especially excited either." Two years ago Jean became involved in a teacher research network by chance, after a colleague invited her to attend a meeting. She found the discussions stimulating and was surprised to find that what teachers discovered about themselves and their students as learners had credibility. With a colleague, she began to explore her own teaching and to keep day-by-day notes. These she shared with her colleague.
>
> Before long Jean found that her approach to teaching was quite different from what it had been. She began to question many of the practices she had followed and generally found new energy and vitality. Three things stand out about her own perceptions about changes in her orientation. First, she notes "I

> notice so many things about children and the ways in which they learn; I talk with children about their learning; it's become a kind of joint venture." Second, she says that she no longer feels comfortable blindly following the curriculum, and she is "especially annoyed when outsiders come in with their solutions for my children who aren't progressing as well as they should. I know more about them than they do; I interact with them all the time." Third, a classroom problem becomes a research problem. "At one time I relied only on what other people wrote and told me; I think I have a few things to say myself now."

Jean represents the voice of a new professionalism, a voice of optimism and confidence. She sees the decisions about children's learning as interesting challenges that she and children face together. She and the children are the key players. Jean is in the process of redefining her role as a teacher, as a learner, as an educator. Central to that redefinition is her role as an astute observer of children, the basis on which learning problems are identified and solved. Third, Jean is excited about the possibility of sharing some of her classroom research through a network newsletter. She feels that what she is learning is worth sharing.

That sentiment is gaining a strong foothold in many places, and promises new beginnings in true professionalism. W. Braun puts it this way:

> The movement [Teacher as Researcher] appears to be generated by us, the teachers. That is new and exciting. The movement is about us as learners, as generators of knowledge about learning and about children. It is motivated, at least in part, by the challenge of a new search for paradigms for thinking about learning and school. Certainly, we have matured to the point where we know that personal reflections about our learning and the learning of children have a legitimate place (1991: i).

Teacher as Interpreter of Information

As mentioned earlier, a typical outcome of traditional assessment schemes was the creation of performance profiles. These were often represented visually in dips and peaks. Even when comparisons were completely untenable, it was assumed that these profiles provided us with quick, logical signals of what to teach. The visual displays of scores were often complemented with a listing of strengths and weaknesses. Hopefully more and more teachers will recognize the flaws in such limiting forms of observation and their loosely corresponding links to instruction. To illustrate:

> Mark, a low-achieving second grader new to his school, was given a battery of tests, as his parents expressed deep concern that he was having reading problems. His profile showed that he was weak in interpretive comprehension, inferential comprehension, and vocabulary, and strong in word identification skills. On the basis of this information, an intensive "comprehension" program was prescribed. The program involved reading short passages and answering questions. Although she was dismayed by it, the classroom teacher was reluctant at first to resist the program prescribed by the learning resource teacher who had conducted the assessment. However, she demanded access to Mark's tests and explained to the learning resource teacher that the results conflicted with what she had observed on a day-to-day basis. After long discussions with both the learning resource teacher and parents, the teacher was able to convince them that on the basis of the information she had collected through close observation and conferences with Mark, the test results pointed to completely erroneous directions for Mark's instruction and learning.

Mark's teacher has learned to avoid thinking in terms of profiles, especially profiles derived from sources that leave too many unanswered questions. What she presents to other professionals and parents is much closer to a script, a scenario that demonstrates the kinds of strategies that children use under particular kinds of instructional conditions. Her task is much more demanding than that of one who follows prescriptions. Not only must she observe children in a range of circumstances, but she must constantly interpret the information as she creates a kind of mental mapping of the child's abilities, constantly changing and suggesting new observational needs and new instructional challenges. Even the probing is interpretive, as Mickelson (1985) has pointed out. This kind of information-gathering about learners and the ongoing sorting is an interpretive act of the highest order. Stierer puts it this way:

> Coming to know a reader is, after all, a case of making meaning within a complex social context. ... [This] sociolinguistic emphasis makes explicit two aspects of reading assessment. First, it reinforces the sense-making nature of assessment, in contrast with the widely held belief that it is an unambiguous mechanical operation. Second, it locates the assessment process within a situation which comprises a complex network of social structures and relationships (1983: 81).

In other words, the teacher is no longer the passive receiver of information; she is the generator of information based on everything that she hears and sees in her day-to-day dealings with children. Of course, other professionals may still be consulted. What changes is the direction of information flow when other professionals must be consulted. At the very least, the flow of information becomes bidirectional. Generally the teacher who has the really critical information and questions initiates discussion. Ideally relationships become based on cooperative problem solving—in a setting when professionals keep stretching their abilities and children receive instruction based on foolproof observational information. A vital part of that observation focuses on the kinds of instructional strategies that help the learner develop new ones and apply existing ones.

Thinking about ourselves as legitimate observers and interpreters is critical for our growth as professionals. The engagements we find ourselves in, the talking we do with colleagues as a result, and the reflections that come from it all lead us to think of our roles and responsibilities in new ways. New questions emerge from "our teaching and our interactions with others" (Short 1990: 29). Expanding knowledge, new insights about self, children, and schooling are central. Harris puts it well:

> Science and philosophy do not advance, as people commonly suppose, by finding answers to problems as much as by discovering that the questions they are asking are wrong or inappropriate. (If you are asking the wrong questions, there is no way you are going to get the right answer.) (1986: 17)

Zone of Proximal Development: Stretching the Limits of Teacher Competence

At the risk of repeating what may be common knowledge for many, I will summarize Vygotsky's "zone of proximal development" framework; draw some examples to illustrate how the framework applies in reading assessment, learning, and instruction; then reflect on this framework as a day-to-day stimulus to stretch one's thinking about learning. While the concept of zones has been discussed as a context for stretching children's learning, I argue that such stretching applies first to teachers, and then to children.

The zone of proximal development is defined as:

> ... the distance between the actual developmental level as determined by independent problem solving, and the level of potential development as determined through problem solving under adult guidance or in collaboration with more capable peers (Vygotsky 1978: 86).

This has many implications for our thinking about children's actual development. In a typical test situation, the assumption is made that the child's "level" can be determined by what he can do independently. We never know if he just barely missed a solution, used reasonable strategies to approach the problem and just missed the final answer, or missed by a mile. From an instructional standpoint, this leaves an informational void. When the teacher and child chart zones of development, however, they can observe directly how much and what kind of guidance is required to reach a solution. If, for example, a child is unable to answer a problem himself but is able to do so (either independently or in collaboration with peers) if the teacher initiates the solution, the child's first attempt is not indicative of his actual developmental level. He is somewhere in the zone between the actual and the potential developmental levels. The implications for learning development are that:

> ...learning awakens a variety of internal development processes that are able to operate only when the child is interacting with people in his environment and in cooperation with his peers. Once these processes are internalized, they become part of the child's independent developmental achievement (Ibid. 1978: 90).

Observation in this sense means teachers need to look and listen while the conditions for learning are undergoing change. This is interpretive observation in the truest sense. Teachers must become knowledgeable through constant observation of the child's zones. Only as children are placed in contexts where they operate within these zones will they "display the most instructionally useful information about their learning" (Johnston 1992: 46).The teacher's task is to create environments in which children operate within these zones and then stretch their own limits to determine the contexts and instructional activities that will push children to the "cutting edge of learning." It is this cutting edge that becomes the child's new actual developmental level. An important aspect of the agenda is to "help a child to know what it feels like to learn within the zone of proximal development" (Ibid.: 50). Equally important, this approach constantly points the child to new possibilities as a learner;

it directs the teacher to new possibilities and potentials in instruction. Further, an environment in which "shared completion"—completion of tasks by child and teacher or by a group of children—is not only acceptable but the norm, stimulates children to take risks. Such an environment exposes potential that would otherwise remain hidden to both child and teacher.

Clay's view is that the zone of proximal development concept reminds us to ask the right questions relevant to a given task: "How do we know whether he has any more to give? And if he has, how do we reach towards it?" (Ibid.: 65). She has some pertinent advice. First, if all children are assigned the same task, we are not testing the zone of proximal development of either the most competent or the least competent. Second, if children are presented with simple, unchallenging tasks, we have no opportunity to observe the wide range and variety of individual ways of responding because all children will perform successfully. "The essence of successful teaching is to know where the frontier of learning is for any one pupil on a particular task" (Ibid.). Moreover instructionally limiting settings do not invite the teacher to observe the potential of children. Such settings stifle learning for both child and teacher. An illustration follows:

> Ursula, a six-year-old child, has had considerable exposure to books even before she arrived at school. From observing the child's involvement with text, the teacher sees that Ursula understands many of the basic concepts about print: she knows that both print and picture combine to carry the text message; she knows where text on the page begins and the direction in which print proceeds on the page; she is aware of the correspondence between words in print and their spoken counterparts, though not necessarily on a one-to-one match; she recognizes some words, especially words from her immediate environment but also some words of particular interest to her from the literature she has been exposed to (for example, *gingerbread, Goldilocks, Snow White, dinosaur*). These understandings represent part of Ursula's actual developmental level.
>
> Recently Ursula's teacher has noticed some frustration. Ursula is trying to read some of the pieces of text that she is familiar with, some that she has memorized. Ursula reads along, trying to match individual words in print with her spoken words (voice pointing) and typically discovers that she either runs out of text or else runs out of spoken words before she reaches the end of the text. Close observation reveals that Ursula often skips over short words like *a* and *in* without voice pointing. Often polysyllabic words will warrant two or three pointings. Ursula's teacher is now pushed to look for the kinds of expert and/or peer assistance that will assist Ursula in shared completion of a reading task.

> Observations from past performance, of course, are the basis for hypotheses for supportive, shared learning tasks.
>
> Since Ursula has had some success in matching specific words of interest from transcriptions of her own experiences to their spoken counterparts, this is where the teacher begins. Ursula, who loves the story "The Gingerbread Man," is able to repeat with ease the refrain, "Run, run as fast as you can; You can't catch me...." The teacher writes the refrain in large script on individual word cards. Together they assemble the text using a pocket chart to display the newly formed text. Each time the correct word card is located, they say the word and put it in its place. After that they read the text together as Ursula points to the individual word cards. Ursula suggests that she try this on her own. However, as she has some problem identifying specific words, the teacher suggests that Ursula follow the text in the story as she assembles individual cards and reads them. Two tries and Ursula is able to assemble the text on her own. Her comment: "Long words are words and short words are words." What a marvelous insight! Ursula and the teacher discover that she can do short pieces of text independently the next day, but is also very actively engaged when she does larger pieces with one of her friends. To help Ursula gain control of her new discovery, the teacher also encourages her to share a variety of caption books. It isn't long before Ursula is frequently heard saying, "Oh, I know that word, it starts the same as *poodle*," and so on.

Ursula's zone is moving. That is, what used to be her potential level (what she was able to do with support) is now at the outside limit of her developmental level. She has learned how the system works and is able to use it to move on to new learning. She is now free to operate on individual words as she refines what she knows about print/speech relationships. In this case using cards for the words allows both teacher and child to talk freely about what they are doing. It also allows the child more freedom to take risks. There is nothing to erase or cross out; she simply has to replace a word card as she tests one against other possibilities. The manipulative aspect of the exercise is likely to generate easier talk than an exercise that is more abstract.

There is no formula. The teacher sees and hears, and then makes judgments as to what will help, first in observing where the child's developmental level is, and second, in thinking of appropriate instructional/contextual options—options that can be tested to identify the "cutting edge of learning."

Exploring and testing zones open the doors, then, to real inquiry. They open the doors to discoveries that will no doubt surprise and sometimes shock both child and teacher. They create the setting for what Neilsen calls an "open stance" to "authentic inquiry," a "stance that assumes that the nature of life is constantly evolving and indeterminate..." (1990: 5). Neilsen believes that it is this stance that protects us from "becoming trapped by our existing beliefs/experience to the point where we see what we want to see and hear what we want to hear" (Ibid.). More specifically Graves says that at times the zones of children and teachers overlap and that learning has occurred for both. "That is the celebratory side of teaching and learning" (1991: 140). My guess is that the better the teacher, the more often this will be the case—cause for many celebrations! I like Goodman's statement: "Whole language evaluation plumbs the limits of both teachers and children" (1989: xii). I offer a few questions we may want to ask ourselves as we think about our roles in discovering with children where their zones lie, and the creativity with which we assist them to traverse these zones:

➤ Do I listen in on children as they talk to one another about their learning, and especially as they try to solve a problem?

➤ Do I push children to offer their suggestions as to how to proceed instead of jumping in too early with my suggestions? Am I prone to jump in too soon, especially with children who are already having problems learning to read and write?

➤ Do I engage children in constant monitoring of their own learning, and do I place expectations on them to come up with solutions and justifications for solutions?

➤ Do I encourage children to talk about proposed solutions to the problems; to experiment with solutions individually, and in pairs or groups?

➤ Do I ensure availability of a wide range of materials: sufficient easy material to gain increasing control and fluency; challenging materials that create anomalies and perplexities to uncover the surprises about learnings that are at the "cutting edge"?

➤ Do I incorporate a wide range of experiences to uncover information about children's learning—shared reading (with me and peers), choral reading, reader's theater (observing the reading of a range of parts), reading to revise and edit independently and cooperatively, reading to find out "how to do things," and so on?

➤ For children with special learning problems, do I have a systematic approach to sharing information with colleagues and other professionals so that together we are able to talk about a child's zones in a productive manner, and to share insights about an ever-increasing range of instructional strategies that enable the child to traverse his zones?

➤ In cases where ESL children or others spend part of their instructional time with other professionals, do I establish systematic ways to share observational information and to coordinate our instructional strategies?

➤ Are my observations sensitive to conditions that promote independent reading, and am I alert to conditions that keep the child from pursuing reading?

➤ Do my observations relate to areas of strategy as opposed to inventories of skills?

➤ Do my interactions with children push the frontiers of their own understandings of themselves as learners? Do I encourage thinking triggered by questions such as "How do you know that is correct?" "Are there other ways that you could use to solve the problem?" "What kinds of questions do you want to ask me to help you find out?" "Can you explain to Jody how you discovered the solution?" "Do you think this will work every time?"

Explaining to the Public: Stretching Toward New Insights, New Clarification, New Confidence

As teachers' authority and control over assessment increase, so do expectations that teachers will explain children's learning not only to children but to the public, and especially to parents. There are many advantages to this. First, it avoids the funneling of information about "problem learners" through multiple channels; for example, psychologist to learning resources teacher to classroom teacher and, ultimately, to the parent. It certainly holds the potential for the teacher to assume center stage. Second, over the long-term, this kind of responsibility pushes the teacher to explore ever-increasing ways of observing children's learning and greater collaboration with the child. Third, this new responsibility creates settings in which teachers are expected to explain specific links between observations and instruction. This can develop into discussion of what happens at home and at school so that learning in the two settings might complement each other. We have long known that talking and explaining are ways not only to communicate but also to clarify personal information. I was told recently by a teacher that "we need much more experience in talking about and rationalizing what we're doing; somehow these experiences clarify concepts about learning, but they also help us become more confident using clear, understandable language to explain learning to self and others. We need to convince ourselves first, and then the public." There is a lot of truth in that statement.

In chapter 3 I mentioned the parental pressure my daughter experienced. This was largely because the instruction her first-grade children were getting was too far removed from parents' memories of their own school experience for them to understand or trust. She writes, "By February, pressure from parents was too great to withstand. I felt tired and discouraged. ...I used more energy to respond to parents than I used for teaching my kids" (W. Braun 1985: 45). With the support of the principal, she invited parents not only of her children but also parents of the other first-grade classes to a presentation—there was some feeling that teaching in those classes had been "infected" as well. She spent many, many hours preparing for the presentation. During the course of this preparation she became more and more aware of the reasons for much of what she was doing in her classroom. She found the language to explain to herself and others what she was doing and why. Most significant, since this was her first year as a grade-one teacher, much of what she was doing fit only in the most general sense into a cohesive set of beliefs about children and learning. What this exercise pushed her to do was review more intensively than ever the many exciting things that children had accomplished as readers and writers in less than six months. By the time she was ready for the presentation she writes, "I was more and more convinced that I was on the right track" (Ibid.: 46). She then explained how she gained the confidence of the parents, proving to them the careful observation and thoughtfulness that had gone into the creation of instructional environments for their children:

> The parents laughed when I showed them a poem written in Mandarin [Chinese] and asked them to read it.... I explained how at the beginning of the year, many of the children were bewildered by all the words they saw. Like the parents looking at the Chinese characters, some children weren't sure whether to read from right to left or from top to bottom. Their confusion was natural. Had

> I pushed the children into learning isolated parts without a firm understanding of how the whole system worked, the children would have become confused and lost interest (Ibid.: 47).

In the scenario above, many would have considered it logical to call upon a consultant, program specialist, or supervisor to explain a program that could be understood and rationalized by only one person—the teacher. Teachers who find themselves in situations where they have to explain a position, such as their stand on assessment and teaching, are going to learn much in the sorting-out process. These stretching exercises build strong professional muscles, because underlying all the exercise is an ongoing assessment of what children are doing, *and* what the teacher herself is doing in response—strong winds beneath the wings of teacher change. At the same time, these exercises build teacher self-confidence and credibility in the community.

If we are interested in creating conditions in which teachers are willing to risk change, beginning teachers must know they are expected to explain and defend their approaches to assessment and instruction. The kinds of "instructional histories" (Clandinin 1986) they develop early in their careers (especially the histories rooted in controlling philosophies like those governing basal reading series) limit the need to observe and to think through instruction creatively. Teachers have traditionally defended their instructional practices by focusing on their use of "appropriate" materials, or more often, on the child's inability to apply himself properly. The defense lies less in the observational and instructional expertise of the teacher, and more in the child's attitudes, abilities, and motivation. In such instances, if we expect to be seen as professional, ongoing learners, the focus resides in the wrong place.

In addition to responsibility, however, we need a collaborative spirit and strong support from administrators, consultants, and supervisors. These are the people who are accountable for teacher competence and, ultimately, for their career stability and security. Cochrane-Smith (1991), in her approach to creating conditions in which beginning teachers risk "teaching against the grain," makes a plea for a "collaborative resonance"—a link between what student teachers learn at university with what they learn from their school experiences. As a result of this "co-labor of learning communities, students and teachers alike will critique the culture of teaching and schooling, research their own practice, articulate their own expertise, and call into question the policies and language of schooling that are taken for granted" (Ibid.: 283). Cochrane-Smith notes that "teaching is fundamentally a political activity in which every teacher plays a part, either by design or by default....teachers are decision-makers and collaborators who must reclaim their roles in the shaping of practice by taking a stand as both educators and activists" (Ibid.: 280).

Portfolios and Things: Assessment to Inform Instruction

USING PORTFOLIOS TO GUIDE LEARNING AND INFORM PARENTS

There have been attempts in the last decade to move toward closer alignment between assessment for accountability and assessment for informing instruction. That goal can be achieved only if experimentation continues at the classroom level. Boomer underlines this notion:

> The challenge to school systems is how to be properly accountable about students' capability and performance; responsible and useful in reporting to students, parents and employers; and educationally non-toxic in terms of effect on the integrity of the curriculum and the teaching process. In addition, we need to devise methods of assessment which are "socially just," without cultural or other biases" (1990: 2).

Johnston talks about teachers and children leaving "productive trails of literate activity" (1992: 128). There are many ways in which such trails can be produced and organized. For example, Laura Jacobson, a third-grade teacher, asks her children to keep track of "What I Have Discovered About My Learning" and then document their "discoveries" with examples. These entries are discussed on a regular basis. Stan's entries included, "I know how to use qotation marks in my writing. It works all the time if I listnen to sounds I make in reading. I think I lerned this as we did the readers theter about Hattie and the Fox." Stan documented his discovery with two examples of writing where he demonstrated that he, indeed, knew how to use quotation marks.

As Graves points out, portfolios were common in other fields long before they were considered in education. In education we use them to display important information about the learner's accomplishments—to "display depth at the point of our strengths" (Graves 1991: 19). Teale (1990) places the various strategies for gathering portfolio information on a continuum, with informal observations at one end and test results at the other. Many would resist the notion of using test information in devising the "paper trail" —particularly if the purpose of the portfolio is to inform learning and instruction as well as to achieve accountability.

Graves (1991) provides a set of guidelines for conceptualizing the notion of portfolios. They start with the teacher and child actively collaborating in selecting the best three papers the child has written in an eight-week period (a period Graves considers reasonable for younger children). This collection provides an opportunity to "make the best better." It helps children become aware of their "experiments and specialties." If the work consists of only one genre of writing, it raises the question of what the child should work on next—what areas they may want to experiment with or work at in greater depth. Portfolios are seen as a stimulus for child and teacher to plan future direction.

Johnston (1992) draws some useful distinctions between folders and portfolios, each of which is a tool for organizing paper trails. He views the folder as the first level of work—a collection of documents of ongoing projects. A writing folder, for example, might contain drafts and revisions, pieces set aside to be worked on at a later time, some pieces in the process of revision of editing, flexible plans for future writing, a list of books already published. It might include learning logs, personal response journals, and observation notes. It is, as Johnston says, a working folder.

Less is said in the literature about reading folders than about writing folders. These should be given as much credence as writing folders. The resourcefulness of both teacher and child is the only limitation on what these would contain. A reading folder could include documentation of books read, a list of readings shared with groups of children (and/or adults), logs about both the development of tastes as well as strategies, pieces of favorite verse and reader's theater pieces that the child hopes to refine, and so on. As with the writing log, it is useful for children to have "in-process" reading pieces that they hope to perfect orally. Recording a child's oral reading over a period of time allows both teacher and child to review progress. These logs must be well organized, with a written listing of pieces recorded with corresponding dates and tape footage. It is informative to include notes from both teacher and child. These would comment on the quality of representative pieces, how the reading is changing, and the teaching and learning strategies that are being used to effect these changes. Modified miscue analysis forms, with analytical comments from both child and teacher, may accompany this. These forms may be restricted to a listing of words a child has substituted for words in pieces of text, self-corrections, words omitted and inserted. In its simplest form, the analysis might show whether substitutions, omissions, and so on, typically leave the meaning intact, or whether meaning is distorted by these changes. Alternatively, samples of running records (Clay 1991) could be used (see pages 141–146).

According to Johnston, the portfolio represents selections from the working folders. Two or three times each year (perhaps more frequently for younger children) child and teacher put together a portfolio that can be used as a public statement about the child's development. Depending on the age of the child, these folios might include

- a piece of writing from its draft form to its published form
- samples of a range of genres (letters, verses, and so on) written for a range of audiences and purposes
- records of books read
- writing that illustrates critical thinking about pieces of reading
- demonstrations of developing strategies in both reading and writing (for example, two samples of a child's writing—one showing a dull, banal beginning to a piece; the second one demonstrating a lead designed to captivate the reader)
- a list of pieces published and readings performed
- pieces that integrate reading or writing with art and/or music; documentation of what has been learned in the process
- reflections about "myself as learner"; on "what I'm doing, where I'm going, and how I'm getting there"
- reader notes that accompany the reading of a story, monologue, or reader's theater part that provide some evidence of growing ability to listen to oneself and to adjust learning accordingly
- a recorded interview with a peer about some aspect of language learning, a "status" statement
- letter to the parent or teacher summarizing the portfolio contents, with accompanying "future plans"

Portfolio contents and format vary with the tastes and style of children and teacher. Tierney et al. emphasize that "portfolios should grow from the students' work, interests, and the projects and activities pursued by the class" (1991: 45). Johnston stresses the need for writing to be a reflective self-evaluation. This might be structured with a series of questions from the teacher such as:

- What has changed most about your reading (writing)?
- Why do you think this has changed?
- What change would you like to see in your reading (writing)?
- How do you plan to make that change?
- What is the hardest part of reading (writing) for you?

Clearly the orientation of portfolios places much of the responsibility for choice, and defense of choice, on the child. Certainly this promotes a reflective approach toward monitoring one's own learning and to finding solutions to the everyday problems that arise. As Johnston notes, this promotes a historical stance. Children become "aware that their concerns now [their insecurities of growing up and the level of skill with which they sometimes become frustrated] do in fact pass" (1992: 134).

He maintains that this promotes personal growth and the development of a more grounded personal identity. Significantly children have a basis for reflection on what their successes can be attributed to. That leads to questions such as "What really helped me become fluent?" or "What enabled me to improve in my ability to revise and edit effectively?" This ability to reflect adds an ongoing dimension to the child's thinking about his own learning and that of others with whom he associates daily. It takes the focus off competition with others. By reflecting on where he is coming from and by planning where he is going, he is more inclined to consult with others than to compete with them. The chances for increased consultation are considerable as he finds increasing numbers of questions that he is struggling with.

If the portfolio is used either to complement or supplant the report card, the teacher will want to add pieces to the portfolio. My suggestion is that these pieces become an appendix to what is first and foremost the child's portfolio, not the teacher's. Johnston states that these additions might illustrate aspects of learning development that the child at this stage is unable to see. They provide a way to point the child in a new direction or even help him become aware of an aspect of learning that occurs at an intuitive level, an aspect the teacher realizes can be brought under control and consciously recognized. The teacher might contribute opinions about the child's zones and describe plans for helping children move specific strategies from the actual developmental level "into the zone."

Two examples illustrate possibilities for teacher's additions. Tinu, a second grader, has displayed in his portfolio a series of twenty-three photographs taken on a recent trip. These photographs represent a clear sequence of events. In addition, Tinu has recorded a talk to accompany the photographs. His teacher appended an interpretation of Tinu's work:

> Tinu's display and the accompanying tape represent a quantum leap in his ability to order events, and especially in his ability to elaborate on details. His earlier reports were for the most part stilted and stripped of any interesting detail. He makes his trip come alive with the spirit of presentation, the obvious joy of doing things with his family, and his interesting choice of words to describe places and events. What strikes me most is Tinu's demonstration of subtle humor in his report. His project reveals to me some stunning language breakthroughs. We are going to capitalize on these in his reading, especially since both Tinu and the class celebrated the project together. Tinu has never felt better in his seven years. I share his joy.

Charlene is a first grader who recently started moving from reading memorized text (mostly short four- to five-word lines of verse) to confident finger/voice matching as she reads longer pieces. Concurrently she has started to slow down in some of her reading as she approaches certain words. Charlene has decided that she wants examples of her former reading and "new reading" shown in her portfolio—a challenge for the teacher, who fortunately kept carefully written notes on Charlene's progress. She decided to show Charlene's progress in this manner:

Charlene's earlier reading:

C's finger here C's voice here

Snap, snap went the crackers

C's finger here C's voice here

Whoosh, whoosh went the balloons

Charlene now reads:

Hippety hop to bed

I would rather stay up instead

Charlene reads d-a-dd-eee

But when daddy says must

There is nothing but just

Charlene reads h-h-hipp-p-e-ty

Go hippety hop to bed.

Her finger and voice match every word in the selection. Charlene's teacher appends this note:

> Charlene has made unusual progress as she in a very short while has managed to monitor her movement across lines of print. She is very confident about her ability to match speech to print on a one-to-one basis. What is most remarkable is how quickly she has decided to look inside words that she knows by heart (for example, *daddy, hippety*). This demonstrates a growth spurt while on the surface it may appear regressive. Charlene is suddenly aware of new ways in which print works.

Another part of the teacher's contribution might be an ongoing question/response log that documents children's growth in strategic thinking. This might include, among other things, changing responses to questions such as the following:

- How do you know that's correct?
- Are there other ways to help you figure this out?
- How will this (new reading or listening strategy) help you in your writing?
- Are there other times when you need to use this strategy?
- How could you change your voice to let the listener know that the character is joking?

(Braun and Goepfert 1989: 158)

Finally, the choices that both child and teacher make constitute excellent bases for conferences. It will add to the child's knowledge about himself as a learner; it will uncover for the teacher some of the child's perceptions about himself as learner as well as personal knowledge about her teaching.

The use of portfolios places assessment right in the center of all that is happening in the classroom—and beyond. Used appropriately, portfolios demand constant attention to every aspect of learning and instruction. There is no right or wrong way to create portfolios. There is no formula, nor should there be one. The classroom portfolios that children develop should be as distinctive as the portfolio of the professional artist, musician, or journalist. Teachers and children create.

For children, portfolios provide an excellent place for personal reflection, a way for them to compare where they are now as learners with where they were earlier. And children need concrete evidence that they are progressing. As they compare tapes of earlier reading with current reading, or a piece written in September with another one written in December, they have occasion to celebrate. They can see not only overall changes but also answers to questions like "Am I really getting better at using interesting words in my writing?" and "Am I really getting closer to standard spellings without a lot of support?" From these reflections come a newly found confidence, new energy to move ahead. As Samantha, a seven-year-old, recently said after reviewing her portfolio with her teacher, "I can read lots and lots; I can read hard books now; I can write, and I can change my writing now. I'm good." There is a strong link between a child's *I cans* and *I wills*.

For the teacher, these collections become a necessary mirror in which to see herself as a teacher and learner—her children's portfolios are really portfolios of her teaching. Individual portfolios become the basis for future instruction for children in the class; the composite portfolio acts as a guide for some general planning.

For example, if the teacher sees that most or all of the children have been exposed to a narrow range of genres in both reading and writing, that is a cue for future plans. The teacher may see that many children require more help in their editing than she had expected; mini-lessons are in order for these children. It may not necessarily be a call for a frontal attack on editing; it may be only that some children don't recognize themselves as writers. Graves reminds us that while we may see from children's portfolios the need to experiment with an increasing range of genres, "experimentation does not work unless you are demonstrating how you experiment with new kinds of writing yourself" (1991: 169). Again, child growth and teacher growth move in tandem on parallel tracks.

Portfolios provide an excellent means to both aid in refining and guiding learning and instruction and prove to the public that learning is taking place. In this respect, accountability goes beyond a simple reporting of levels and scores to describing the ways learners have gone about achieving success—the essence of true accountability. Portfolio assessment provides a stage to demonstrate perceptions about process as well as a display of selected artifacts.

The use of portfolios still faces skepticism and criticism. I too have a few cautions and concerns. *Portfolio* has become a buzzword. There are schools and school systems where portfolios are mandated, often with little more preparation than a quick-and-dirty "how-to" workshop. That means that for teachers in those places portfolios have already become an orthodoxy that is not fully understood. That's too bad. If we short-circuit the process and try to make it easy, those teachers will never realize what powerful assessment tools portfolios can be. I have already said there is no formula for the best portfolio; by definition, each has to be distinctive. That spells hard work for both child and teacher. That means constant thinking and rethinking about what best reflects learning, as well as effective yet manageable recording systems.

I believe that a breakthrough in assessment, learning, and instruction resides in the kinds of decisions that teachers and children make about format and contents in the creation of portfolios. Given intelligent use, patience, and trust on the part of administrators and the public, portfolios can narrow the gap between assessment for accountability and assessment to inform learning and instruction. Further, the portfolio is a natural vehicle for teacher professional development. Portfolios at their best are working drafts, ongoing experiments among children and teachers. The ultimate test to determine whether portfolio use will take the route of other educational bandwagons and "clutter the dump" or survive to contribute substantively to educational change depends on teacher persistence and administrative and parental trust. I agree wholeheartedly with Wollman-Bonilla when she says, "Teachers must become comfortable with the feelings of uncertainty and loss-of-control that experimentation can engender" (1991: 115). There is much uncertainty about portfolios. One question is whether or not we can live with that uncertainty. Another is whether or not we can make the long-term commitment to use portfolios not only as an assessment tool, but as a tool to bring about teacher/school change. Lamme (1991) provides a case study of a school where that has happened, albeit within a rather conservative framework. Hansen (1992) also outlines a school experience that informs and gives credibility to the concept of portfolios as an avenue of pupil and teacher growth. It's a beginning—

a very sound beginning. Portfolios could well be instrumental in forging closer links among assessment, learning, and instruction.

BAND PROFILES

From time to time educators have experimented with profiles—ways of showing student learning—to document student achievement. The purpose has always been to develop a more comprehensive picture of student achievement and abilities than is possible using more traditional methods of assessment. What many of these new approaches share is an attempt to show a greater diversity of indicators of children's learning. With this diversity comes more flexibility and greater reliance on teacher observation.

In one of the more promising examples I am aware of, the School Programs Division of the Ministry of Education in Victoria (Australia) has developed the concept of literacy profiles to help teachers "build up a comprehensive picture of students' literacy development." These profiles represent an innovative approach to assessment—teachers are encouraged to observe and record indicators of growth "within the context of everyday classroom activities." What is telling about the thinking behind these profiles is shown in "Putting Our Faith in Teachers," a section of the accompanying *Literary Profiles Handbook* that attests to the responsibility and control that is placed in the laps of teachers.

The actual profiles consist of bands of indicators of achievement, scaled to describe a developmental progression that teachers can use to record their students' literacy development. The profiles are designed to show several qualities: achievements, attitudes, and skills, the assessment of one quality by a number of methods. As an example, Reading Band A (see figure 4.1, page 78) begins with the category "Concepts About Print," which refers to book handling knowledge. The "Reading Strategies" category includes such aspects as locating lines, words, spaces, and identifying familiar words. "Responses" and "Interests and Attitudes" include joining in stories and choosing books as a free time activity. It might be that a child for whom Band A is most descriptive of his emergence as reader may already exhibit behaviors in Band B, such as "uses pictures for clues to meaning of text." Profiles are detailed from levels A through H providing indicators for progressively more advanced readers. Presently the indicators are restricted to reading and writing. However, profiles for oral language observation are being developed.

Fig. 4.1 Literacy Profile

Name ______________________ Date ______________

READING BAND A

☐ **Concepts About Print**

- ☐ Holds book the right way up.
- ☐ Turns pages from the front to the back.
- ☐ On request, indicates the beginning and end of sentences.
- ☐ Distinguishes between upper- and lower-case letters.
- ☐ Indicates the start and end of books.

☐ **Reading Strategies**

- ☐ Locates words, lines, spaces, letters.
- ☐ Refers to letters by name.
- ☐ Locates own name and other familiar words in a short text.
- ☐ Identifies known, familiar words in other contexts.

☐ **Responses**

- ☐ Responds to literature (smiles, claps, listens intently).
- ☐ Joins in familiar stories.

☐ **Interest and Attitudes**

- ☐ Shows preference for particular books.
- ☐ Chooses books as a free time activity.

READING BAND B

☐ **Reading Strategies**

- ☐ Takes risks when reading.
- ☐ "Reads" books with simple repetitive language patterns.
- ☐ Uses pictures for clues to meaning of text.
- ☐ Asks others for help with meaning and pronunciation of words.
- ☐ Consistently reads familiar words and interprets symbols within a text.
- ☐ Predicts words.
- ☐ Matches known clusters of letters to clusters in unknown words.
- ☐ Uses knowledge of words in the environment when "reading" and "writing."
- ☐ Recognizes base words within other words.
- ☐ Names basic parts of a book.
- ☐ Makes a second attempt at a word if it doesn't sound right.

☐ **Responses**

- ☐ Selects own books to "read."
- ☐ Describes connections among events in texts.
- ☐ Writes, role plays, and/or draws in response to a story or other form of writing (e.g., poem, message).
- ☐ Creates ending when the text is left unfinished.
- ☐ Recounts parts of text in writing, drama, or art work.
- ☐ Retells using language expressions from reading sources.
- ☐ Retells with approximate sequence.

READING BAND C

☐ **Reading Strategies**

- ☐ Rereads a paragraph or sentence to establish meaning.
- ☐ Uses context as a basis for predicting meaning of unfamiliar words.
- ☐ Reads aloud showing understanding of purpose of punctuation marks.
- ☐ Uses picture cues to make appropriate responses for unknown words.
- ☐ Uses pictures to help read a text.
- ☐ Finds where another reader is up to in a reading passage.

☐ **Responses**

- ☐ Writing and art work reflect understanding of text.
- ☐ Retells, discusses, and expresses opinions on literature, and reads further.
- ☐ Recalls events and characters spontaneously from text.

☐ **Interest and Attitudes**

- ☐ Seeks recommendations for books to read.
- ☐ Chooses more than one type of book.
- ☐ Chooses to read when given free choice.
- ☐ Concentrates on reading for lengthy periods.

OTHER ASSESSMENTS

____

____

(Adapted from *Literacy Profiles Handbook: Assessing & Reporting*, © 1990, Department of School Education, Victoria, Australia.)

The profiles are seen as observation guides for teachers. They do not include everything that teachers might observe, but offer a selection of indicators that "enable teachers to identify points of growth and to record the sort of information necessary for reporting to parents" (p. 3). However, the designers state explicitly that the "profiles locate the assessment of student language learning firmly within a teaching-learning context. Planning for student learning, assessing and observing, recording growth and reporting that information appropriately are viewed as an integrated process" (p. 4). The following features describe the profiles:

- Indicators are framed in positive terms, describing what children *can* do, not what they fail to do.
- Indicators are observable, leaving no guesswork for intention.
- Indicators are based on criteria that are independent of previous achievement and independent of comparisons with others.
- Indicators reflect strategies, responses, and interests and attitudes.
- The bands do not reflect discrete stages. Learners demonstrate some behaviors at both higher and lower levels than the band that generally describes most of their development. Behaviors at lower levels might well be seen as indicators of actual developmental levels; at higher levels, reflections of "edges of learning."
- The bands are clusters of behaviors arranged in broad levels, rather than checklists in which isolated behaviors are seen to take on great significance.
- Indicators are not exhaustive; they leave open the possibility, indeed, the invitation for teachers to add or delete.

These records of student growth provide a synthesis of observations, judgments, and evidence drawn from a variety of sources, such as classroom observation, writing folders or samples, reading logs or journals, running records, and conference notes. They allow teachers to develop a record of literacy growth. In reporting to parents, these profile records may act as prompts, directing the teacher to these other records for evidence and illustration. Again, observation has a dual purpose: to inform learning and instruction and to provide a public record. It has the added advantage of allowing teachers freedom to learn and grow.

The bands in these profiles, then, not only enable teachers to broaden their observations but also to create a picture of the child as a reader and writer. As the teacher experiments and expands her views of learning, new achievement categories will appear in the bands. This open-endedness has great appeal as we attempt to narrow the gap between legitimate observation for accountability purposes and information that is useful to support child learning.

CHECKLISTS

There have been various attempts earlier to enable and encourage teachers to "expand the gaze" in their observations through the use of checklists. Often these checklists have been received with great enthusiasm, used for a short while, and then guiltily abandoned. In light of current approaches to observation/assessment, it is easy to see why these lists have created a massive compost heap. First, they represented a static picture of the learner, and doubtlessly a distorted one as the categories were predetermined and driven by a very narrow view of the reading/writing process. Second, the predetermined prescriptive nature of the checklist did not motivate teacher exploration and problem solving and had little value as a "professional stretcher." The checklist was seen as a way of making observation easier. Third, the checklist often was an end in itself. There was no provision for interpretive analysis and no connection with specific learning/instructional plans. Finally, filling in the checklist was the exclusive domain of the teacher.

I have used extensions of the checklist as a means to bring children and teachers together in collaboration on observation, and to devise on an ongoing basis the indicators (strategy categories) for observation (Braun and Goepfert 1989). Further, the observational data are used by both child and teacher as a basis for reflection and discussion about "attributions for success"; that is, the kinds of assistance and the kinds of personal efforts that have worked for the child. Figure 4.2 illustrates how children are invited to reflect on the strategies they use. The reading checklist in figure 4.3 is a parallel form to be used by the teacher. These are the basis for discussion and continuing observation. Figure 4.4 illustrates how indicators might change as children have progressed beyond the stage reflected by indicators in figures 4.2 and 4.3. There are a number of ways in which these forms can be used to reflect the child's zones in reading development. First, the *often* and *sometimes* categories can be seen as indications where the child is operating at the

Fig. 4.2 Thinking About Myself as a Reader—Sheet 1

Name ______________________________ Date ________________

	Often	*Sometimes*	*Seldom*
I use pictures, titles, and headings to think about my reading.	☐	☐	☐
I think of different reasons for reading.	☐	☐	☐
I try to think of what will come next as I read.	☐	☐	☐
I go back and reread when I don't understand.	☐	☐	☐
I skip hard words and go on to the next part.	☐	☐	☐
I look for hints the author gives.	☐	☐	☐
I try to pick out the most important ideas.	☐	☐	☐
I use different strategies for different kinds of reading.	☐	☐	☐
I try not to think of other things when I am reading.	☐	☐	☐
I ______________________________	☐	☐	☐
I ______________________________	☐	☐	☐

A strategy I will work on is: ______________________________

____

____

____

These are some things I can do to help me with this strategy: ______________________________

____

____

____

My teacher's comments: ______________________________

____

____

____

Name ______________________________ Date ______________

The child:	*Often*	*Sometimes*	*Seldom*
Uses pictures, illustrations, and headings to establish a context for reading.	☐	☐	☐
Sets appropriate purposes for differing types of reading.	☐	☐	☐
Tries to predict what will follow.	☐	☐	☐
Rereads when meaning unclear.	☐	☐	☐
Skips unfamiliar words and reads on.	☐	☐	☐
Is sensitive to author cues.	☐	☐	☐
Tries to select for important information.	☐	☐	☐
Uses a range of strategies, depending on the kind of text.	☐	☐	☐
Tries to summarize what has been said.	☐	☐	☐
Tries to ignore possible distractions and to attend to what is being read.	☐	☐	☐
______________________ ______________________	☐	☐	☐
______________________ ______________________	☐	☐	☐
______________________ ______________________	☐	☐	☐

Teacher's comments: ______________________________

____

____

____

Child's comments: ______________________________

____

____

____

Fig. 4.4 Thinking About Myself as a Reader—Sheet 2

Name ______________________ Date ____________

	Often	*Sometimes*	*Seldom*
I read silently whenever possible.	☐	☐	☐
I read parts aloud when I get confused.	☐	☐	☐
I set a purpose for reading and skip sections that are not helpful.	☐	☐	☐
I apply strategies and acquire new ones in all my reading at school and at home.	☐	☐	☐
I listen to text on the tape recorder to get me started.	☐	☐	☐
I discuss text with others.	☐	☐	☐
I think about what I already know before I start reading.	☐	☐	☐
I read some familiar material every day to gain fluency.	☐	☐	☐
I ______________________	☐	☐	☐
I ______________________	☐	☐	☐

How I feel about my reading: ______________________

A strategy I will work on is: ______________________

My teacher's comments: ______________________

actual developmental level; the *seldom* category, as indications of strategies within the potential developmental level (especially if it is evident that the child requires support to operate within these categories). As teacher and child review the changes over time, the evidence of learning and instruction is well documented. Second, the particular descriptors vary with child and teacher. It may be helpful in fact for both child and teacher to begin with blank forms and gradually add descriptors as learning and teaching progress. The actual descriptors used are of course a clear reflection of the belief system of the teacher. (These will no doubt change over time; in fact it would be interesting for the teacher to keep copies of these records over a period of years to reflect on her own growth.)

The bases for the information used to complete the forms are the in-class activities, conferences, group activities, and so on. Similar observation forms are used for first draft writing, revision/editing, listening, and oral language development (Braun and Goepfert 1989).

The use of collaborative review forms like these opens the doors for teacher and child to plan together for the best kinds of assistance. As the child learns to monitor his learning with the prompting and probing of the teacher, he becomes more reflective of and increasingly in control of his learning. Part of that control involves knowing when to ask for assistance and knowing what kind of assistance he needs—a problem-solving approach to helping himself. The bonus is a well-documented, continuous paper trail as proof of learning and instruction for the public eye.

Concluding Comments

It is doubtful that substantive teacher change is possible in circumstances where assessment for accountability and assessment for informing instruction are at odds. Where teachers are given an unequivocal mandate to integrate instruction and assessment, chances are that teaching is going to undergo dramatic changes. Scharer and Detwiler bring that reality into clear focus:

> As Deana [the teacher] refocused her observations of students away from worksheets, she not only deepened her understanding of her students but also used those observations to confirm changes in her role as teacher and in the students' role as learners (1992: 28).

This ongoing interplay among assessment, learning, and instruction opens the doors to true research in the classroom; it opens the door to the ideal in child and teacher collaboration. Both teacher and child are gatherers of data, both are interpreters of the data. Observation/assessment is at the base of it all.

The zone of proximal development as a basis for observation and instruction holds promise as a way to close the accountability/instructional gap. It pushes the teacher to ongoing observation. It stretches the limits of her potential to create the expert assistance that both defines the zones and assists the learner in moving from his actual developmental level to his potential level.

Assessment practices can and should be reconceptualized. The use of portfolios and "band profiles" offer considerable promise. However, a niggling danger lies in trying to streamline the process. By becoming more efficient, we mandate yet another orthodoxy and that is what we must guard against. It is the ongoing creation borne of observation and instruction/learning that is incentive for teachers to grow professionally—the real "wind underneath the wings of change."

REFERENCES

Braun, C., and P. Goepfert. Strategies. Scarborough, ON: Nelson Canada, 1989.

Braun, W. Editorial, *Calgary and District IRA Newsletter* (Spring 1991): 1.

———. "A Teacher Talks to Parents." *Breaking Ground: Teachers Relate Reading and Writing in the Elementary School*. Edited by J. Hansen, T. Newkirk, and D. Graves. Portsmouth, NH: Heinemann, 1985.

Boomer, G. "Inaugural Newsletter of the Australasian Cooperative Assessment Program" (June 1990).

Clandinin, D. J. *Classroom Practice: Teacher Images in Action*. Bristol, PA: The Falmer Press, 1986.

Clay, M. M. *Becoming Literate: The Construction of Inner Control*. Portsmouth, NH: Heinemann, 1991.

Cochrane-Smith, M. "Learning to Teach Against the Grain." *Harvard Educational Review* 61 (3) August 1991: 279-310.

Goodman, K. S., Y. M. Goodman, and W. J. Wood. *The Whole Language Evaluation Handbook*. Portsmouth, NH: Heinemann, 1989.

Graves, D. H. *Build a Literate Classroom*. Portsmouth, NH: Heinemann, 1991.

Hansen. J. "Literacy Portfolios Emerge." *The Reading Teacher* 45 (8) April 1992: 604-607.

Harris, S. "Strictly Personal." *Times-Colonist* (November 18, 1986).

Johnston, P. H. *Constructive Evaluation of Literate Behavior*. New York: Longman, 1992.

Lamme, L. L., and C. Hysmith "One School's Adventure into Portfolio Assessment." *Language Arts* 68 (December 1991): 629-640.

Literacy Profiles Handbook: Assessing and Reporting. School Programs Division, Ministry of Education, Victoria, Australia, 1990.

Mickelson, N. I. *Evaluation in Whole Language.* Victoria, BC: University of Victoria, 1985.

Neilsen, A.R. "Reflective Teaching As Authentic Inquiry." Annual Meeting of the National Reading Conference. Miami, Florida (December 1990).

Scharer, P. L., and D. B. Detwiler. "Changing As Teachers: Perils and Possibilities of Literature-Based Language Arts Instruction." *Language Arts* 9 (3) March 1992: 186-192.

Short, K. G. "Teachers As Researchers: Classrooms As Communities of Inquiry." *Reading Today* (August/September 1990): 29.

Stierer, B. "A Researcher Reading Teachers Reading Children Reading." In *Opening Moves.* Edited by M. Meck. University of London, UK: Institute of Education, 1983.

Teale, W. H. "The Promise and Challenge of Informal Assessment in Early Literacy." In L. M. Morrow, and J. K. Smith, *Assessment for Instruction in Early Literacy*. 45-61 New York: Prentice Hall, 1990.

Tierney, R. J., M.A. Carter, and L.E. Desai. *Portfolio Assessment in the Reading Writing Classroom*. Norwood, CA: Christopher Gordon Publishers, 1991.

Vygotsky, L. S. *Mind in Society: The Development of Higher Psychological Processes.* Cambridge, MA: Harvard University Press, 1978.

Wollman-Bonilla, J. E. "Shouting from the Tops of Buildings: Teachers As Learners and Change in Schools." *Language Arts* 68 (February 1991): 114-120.

Observation and Assessment in Practice

Assessing Beliefs and Practices That Influence Motivation to Read

5

Just as an athlete's continuing pursuits are fueled by the love of his sport, his beliefs in what the sport can do for him, and his ongoing belief in success, so the young reader's expectations and continued engagements and goals are shaped by his feelings about reading, his hopes, and beliefs in himself. For both athlete and reader, beliefs in long-term success are kept alive by feelings of success in day-to-day activities. With few exceptions love of an activity and success exist in partnership. For athlete and reader alike continued success resides largely in environments that promote excellence and at the same time encourage, respect, and support the learner.

The best guarantee that children will choose reading as a pleasurable alternative to other activities is to provide environments that are conducive to learning. These environments include what practices teachers model as learners themselves, how they structure the classroom, how they interact with children, the materials they promote, and the attitudes they exhibit in day-to-day interactions with children. They include the extent to which support is given to children and the extent to which children are expected to monitor themselves as learners/readers. A classroom environment is anything from the establishment of relationships to how tables and chairs are arranged to facilitate collaboration and cooperation. And all this reflects on teacher beliefs about children and learning.

It is also worth mentioning the home environment. Educators now recognize the importance of parental involvement in a child's literacy development. Teacher and reading specialist Steven Bialostok maintains that all parents should understand the reading process and the importance of their role as "literacy nurturers" (1992: 5). Reading, looking at, and listening to books at home contribute immeasurably to a child's reading success. Talking to parents at parent's night and through home newsletters, and providing books and articles about how they can participate in their child's learning are just some ways to educate and engage them in the process.

In this chapter I look at some of the measures that can be taken to monitor classroom reading environments and the general classroom learning environment to ensure that children will occupy spaces that promote success and confidence—the prerequisites to ongoing love of learning and the motivation to read.

The Classroom as a Reading Environment

Take a close look at the general reading environment in the classroom. Do conditions invite children to approach reading? It has been said, "The person who is able to read but doesn't read has little advantage over the person who can't read." We want skilled readers who are turned on to reading. The difference between conditions that invite and those that repel is often subtle. For that reason, children and teacher must cooperate to ensure that the class is a place where reading not only survives, but thrives.

Let's highlight a few of the conditions that tend to inhibit people from reading. First, we like to do things that we do well. Therefore it is essential that children develop ease and fluency early in their reading lives. Otherwise they will engage in other activities that they find easier and thus more enjoyable, and reading may be perceived as a chore.

To illustrate, for eight months Kia, a third grader, has been with a group of children who have few books that they are able to read with ease. Much of the reading for Kia and others in the group involves plodding along lines of print often unsure of up to 20 percent of the words. The stress this has created has left Kia angry and frustrated. She resists reading even at home where easier books are available. She feels she is a failure, says she's "a no-good reader," and generally has given up. Her main interest at home is watching television; little if anything interests her at school.

Instances like this occur—often without any awareness of the degree to which classroom environments change the lives of children. Kia's teacher was unaware how important it is to have a wide range of books of many genres and levels easily accessible.

Second, "skill, drill, and kill" approaches are unpopular in any area of human endeavor, including reading. Too much unrelated drill and too many questions of the wrong sort are among the things that turn children off, sometimes forever. Michelle Landsberg gives advice to parents that is equally relevant for the classroom:

> If you wanted your child to enjoy athletic activity, would you begin by drilling the baby in the crib with pictures of the different parts of the ski harness? Or would you simply take him along in a backpack... and when he was old enough for skis, you would encourage him to join you, adjusting your pace to suit his pace... The technical knowledge would come through the soles of his feet and the seat of his snowsuit; the motivation to learn would arise from his natural desire to imitate (1986: 20).

Perhaps we can't carry that analogy all the way when we think about school learning, but the idea is excellent. There have been many instances when children's learning was stifled because they were spoon-fed too long by both teacher and parent. To exacerbate the situation, we often filled the spoon with the wrong medicine. The greatest irony is that this continues to be so, especially with children who have already failed. Landsberg's analogy should give pause for self-examination.

Pressures on teachers sometimes create conditions where the emphasis on skill development becomes paramount and the "will" aspect of reading is all but forgotten. That appears to have been the case with Ms. Phillips in the following vignette:

> Ms. Phillips, a third-grade teacher, has been troubled lately by the diminished reading activity of many of her kids. She isn't sure whether or not her imagination, fueled by feelings of guilt, has been playing tricks on her, but she suspects that at least half of her children have reached a plateau in their reading. She is able to report little if any improvement in strategies for thirteen of her twenty-nine children. Further, enthusiasm is low.
>
> Thoroughly perplexed, she confers with Mrs. Sumala, the second-grade teacher, only to discover that most of the children had been enthusiastic readers the year before. In fact, Mrs. Sumala has copies of their reading records.
>
> Ms. Phillips meets regularly with five other teachers to discuss their teach-

> ing and learning strategies. Ms. Phillips raises her problem with the group. They spend the next three sessions talking about feelings about learning—their own and that of children. Ms. Phillips makes careful notes of what the other group members say and takes careful stock of what is happening in her classroom. Upon reflection, she comes to a number of realizations.
>
> First, in preparation for her permanent certification evaluation, her concern for skills has taken over for the past few months. Second, she has been reading less to and with the kids, and has spent less time talking with the kids about their reading. The most surprising realization is that to "de-skill," at least on the surface, she has kept the kids so busy in response journal writing that there is very little time to really get involved in reading. In fact, in her conferences with kids, she discovers that many of them have used book length as their major criterion for book selection for the last few months, choosing books with little print.
>
> What really surprises her, though, is that a few of the children dare to tell her that she has not read as much to them as she used to, and that they miss, as one child puts it, "all listening together while you read such neat stories." This reminds her that some of the children used to borrow books she had read to them to read themselves or to take home for their parents to read to them.

The vignette highlights the need for constant vigilance, the need to step back from time to time so that potentially excellent ideas such as response journal writing don't override common sense. Further, it points out the need for greater trust in wide reading as a means to become a better reader. That reminder has been around for years, but to put it into practice when accountability clouds loom is another matter (Smith 1992). The vignette proves once again that teacher networks have a vital place in helping educators distance themselves to assess their work with children and to see the big picture. Networks can also serve as reminders that children, given the opportunity, can help us get back on track.

One way to create and maintain healthy reading conditions is to conduct periodic examinations of the class environment. Discussions between teacher and children often result in interesting new observations to take into account. The questions raised in figure 5.1, opposite, may be used as a starting point.

Periodic assessments of the environment, especially those involving children and parents, go a long way to promote children's engagement in reading. The greatest payoffs come when competition is kept to a minimum. Environment will remain healthy only if assessment of individual children is based on

Name ______________________________ Date ________________

	Yes	*Maybe*	*No*
I ensure easy access to books and tapes of literature.	☐	☐	☐
– variety	☐	☐	☐
– age-appropriate	☐	☐	☐
I model personal reading of a variety of literature.	☐	☐	☐
I encourage sharing of reading in all kinds of forms: reader's theater, choral reading, and so on.	☐	☐	☐
I emphasize both listening to well-read literature and reading independently.	☐	☐	☐
I work on developing comfortable support systems for students who need support.	☐	☐	☐
We write and talk a lot about reading, how we read and what we are reading, but not at the expense of reading itself.	☐	☐	☐
We talk about the importance of reading in our lives and in the lives of others.	☐	☐	☐
Together we plan ways to make time for reading and ways to assist those in class who need additional support.	☐	☐	☐
I avoid "assignments" that detract from the enjoyment of and involvement with literature.	☐	☐	☐
We discuss reading strategies in the context of every subject area.	☐	☐	☐
I ensure a variety of responses to literature: written, artistic, reader's theater, monologue, drama; sometimes no response at all.	☐	☐	☐
I monitor continuously to ensure that there are no impediments to an individual's reading, such as lack of sufficient fluency, interest, competing pressures, and so on.	☐	☐	☐
I emphasize the development of strategies rather than the aggregation of isolated skills.	☐	☐	☐

Continued

Fig. 5.1 Taking Stock of the Reading Environment—Continued

	Yes	*Maybe*	*No*
I am on the lookout for impediments to self-confidence and threats to "reading self-image" such as competition and other undue pressures.	☐	☐	☐
I make sure that assessment and evaluation don't get in the way of children's engagement in reading and listening. I ask children for input about anything that could get in the way of reading and listening enjoyment.	☐	☐	☐
Other______________________________________	☐	☐	☐
Other______________________________________	☐	☐	☐

Summary of my observations and plans: ______________________________

____

____

____

____

Children's reactions and suggestions: ______________________________

____

____

____

____

Feedback from parents: ______________________________________

____

____

____

____

legitimate literate activities, not contrived exercises (which have only limited relevance to real reading). "The best-laid plans" to promote wide reading will always be subverted unless assessment practices fall clearly into line with the overall goal of promoting wide reading.

Affective and other aspects of learning and instruction are separated in this book for clarity only. In reality, all aspects of learning and instruction must be seen in concert. For example, a child may lose interest in reading (an affective condition) because he has not developed the strategies (cognitive linguistic) he needs to enjoy reading. Why? It may be that strategies necessary to maintain fluency (linguistic strategies) have not kept pace with his need to read interesting pieces (affective aspect). Or it may simply be that the child has not mastered high frequency words to the point of automaticity (a linguistic aspect). More reason for continuing observation.

Monitoring Learning Through Ongoing Assessment

TEACHER SELF-REFLECTION

There is a close tie between a favorable classroom reading environment and the classroom as an overall learning environment. Aspects of the overall environment pervade everything that happens in the classroom. Certain generic aspects of the environment, however, deserve special comment. A sample teacher observation form is helpful for looking at personal beliefs about the overall classroom setting. Figure 5.2 presents a sample form that can be used as a basis for developing a working form, one that can become part of the teacher's personal portfolio.

Filling out a checklist periodically does not guarantee change in behavior. However, when there is a serious desire to look at personal practice such forms can be helpful. This is especially true when colleagues get together to observe one another and then discuss what they have seen. Some teachers exchange their checklists and interview each other. Based on observation of everyday practice they ask them to confirm or refute claims made on the checklist. Videotaping is helpful if teachers don't rely on only one or two tapes; there are too many moment-by-moment developments that can skew the overall picture. Even periodic audiotapes are helpful. They reveal aspects

Fig. 5.2 Assessing the Classroom Teaching / Learning Environment

Name ______________________ Date ______________

	High Priority	*Low Priority*
Positive Learning / Literacy Experiences		
I involve children in decisions.	☐	☐
I give children choices.	☐	☐
I model enthusiasm for learning.	☐	☐
I collaborate with children in planning learning experiences.	☐	☐
I plan for literacy celebrations: publication of pieces, preparing for audience readings, choral readings, and so on.	☐	☐
I set children up for success, and constantly search for new meaning to the rhetoric by experimenting with teaching/assessment interplays.	☐	☐
I take risks and create safe conditions for children's risk taking.	☐	☐
I am learning to take more and more risks myself.	☐	☐
I incorporate music, art, drama with many learning experiences.	☐	☐
I make every attempt to ensure real literacy events, constantly guarding against "dummy runs."	☐	☐

	High Priority	*Low Priority*
Collaborative Learning Climate		
I emphasize support rather than competition.	☐	☐
I invite sharing strategy discoveries.	☐	☐
I group flexibly according to day-to-day needs, talents, and interests, believing that children with divergent abilities and experiences learn from one another.	☐	☐
I encourage support systems of all kinds in my classroom: partner reading, tapes for support, volunteers, and so on.	☐	☐

	High Priority	*Low Priority*
Promoting Self-Improvement Strategies		
I encourage children to reflect on strategies that have worked as they have solved a problem.	☐	☐
I encourage children to talk with each other about strategies that have worked for them.	☐	☐
I emphasize strategy in my ongoing assessment as well as in daily instructional routines.	☐	☐
I model thinking about strategies.	☐	☐
I keep a running written dialogue with children about their progress as strategic learners.	☐	☐
The Place of Assessment in the Curriculum		
Ongoing assessment/observation guides everything we do in class.	☐	☐
Monitoring is both a personal and a collaborative enterprise.	☐	☐
There are no surprises for children in their reports to parents.	☐	☐

Comments: ____

____

____

____

____

____

____

____

____

____

of questioning, forms of encouragement, and true collaborative spirit. Along with teachers' journal entries, ongoing, dated personal checklists like the one in figure 5.2 can become highly productive tools for self-evaluation, a paper trail of personal growth for the teacher's portfolio.

MOTIVATING LEARNERS THROUGH SELF-EXAMINATION

To complement the categories above, I present some sample questions that can be modeled for children to help them develop strategic attacks on problems. The rationale for these questions focuses on strategies that have the potential to give ongoing hope and assurance to both child and teacher. And these qualities are essential to keep motivational energy alive.

➤ How can I anticipate the meaning of this word (paragraph, story)? Does it look as if _________ will happen? Was I correct? How do I know?

➤ Will the rhyme (structure, pattern, and so on) help me to predict and read?

➤ What do I need to know before I continue reading (writing)?

➤ How could this reading strategy help me in my writing?

➤ What did the author do to help me change my mind? How can I use this strategy to convince my readers?

➤ How can I use this webbing strategy in my science reading?

➤ How can I organize my timetable to get more time to listen to music?

➤ What are some things that will improve my listening?

(Braun and Goepfert 1989)

The significance of teachers' involvement in, and concern about, self-examination as part of the whole assessment process is that by taking such a stance they clearly put themselves on center stage as learners along with the children. As one teacher wrote in her journal:

> I am just getting to be comfortable finding categories that are useful in reflecting on myself as a teacher/learner. For a while I just didn't care to look in certain "corners" for fear I would discover something that I'd rather not know about myself. I'm past that since I have discovered that looking at myself (especially

with the help of some of my colleagues) puts me in control of my learning. It's no different than it is for the kids. That's perhaps the most important discovery I've made. If nothing else, it raises my consciousness about things that get in the way of learning, even things that get in the way of wanting to learn.

In addition to the classroom environment records, it is important to continue observing the personal involvement and the development of reading and listening tastes of each child. These observations should include not only the *amount* of reading, but the reading *choices* the child makes. Respect the child's right to go on author binges from time to time—just the way adults do. Ask children to keep personal records of their reading for themselves *and* for their parents. I suggest children keep records of their reading in "reading fun folders" and include in these folders notes about things that they think they want to reread at some time (Braun and Goepfert 1989). They can also put in things like pieces of poetry (their own as well as pieces published by others), reader's theater scripts, favorite choral reading pieces, and so on. The folder is an excellent indicator of what is important to the child and a valuable record of changes in the child's perceptions over time. It is an excellent combination of both a mini-portfolio and a cumulative record.

I also encourage children to list selections from favorite tapes in their folders. This gives listening the kind of prominence it deserves. And children have all kinds of reasons for listing their favorites. One child wrote: "I want to listn to 'if Pigs Coud Fly' agan 'cause I wnt to read it by myslf. I can soon." What a statement of interest and intention!

OBSERVING CHILDREN'S INVOLVEMENT AND ENJOYMENT

Some of the best information about what motivates children and what they enjoy comes from discussions about what you have read to them and with them, from their laughter and weeping, and from their expression of character as they read scripts. This information about what makes them happy or sad will also surface during conferences with the children—one of the best sources of assessment information.

Use a form like the one shown in figure 5.3 to assist but not to formalize observation of individual children's involvement in and enjoyment of reading activities. (Revise it as needed.)

Information entered on the form can be gleaned through conferences as

Fig. 5.3 Observing Reading Involvement and Enjoyment

Name ________________________________ Date __________________

	Often	*Seldom*	*Never*
Selects reading as a diversion	☐	☐	☐
Reads a variety of literature	☐	☐	☐
Likes to talk about books and authors	☐	☐	☐
Responds emotionally to literature read or listened to	☐	☐	☐
Likes to share reading with others	☐	☐	☐
Voluntarily writes about his/her book experiences	☐	☐	☐
Revisits stories or poems from time to time	☐	☐	☐
Approaches reading confidently (oral and silent)	☐	☐	☐
Other ________________________________	☐	☐	☐

____

____

Comments: ________________________________

____

____

____

____

Notes from conference with child: ________________________________

____

____

____

____

Comments from parents: ________________________________

____

____

____

____

well as casual observations of children. In fact, you might find it helpful to append a sheet documenting sources of information (or else leave space on the form itself). Teachers can schedule a small-group or individual conference to talk with children about their observations so that children have an opportunity to add to—or even refute—some of the teacher's information. A significant part of such a conference should deal with children's own perceptions of impediments to their continued reading.

Many inferences can be drawn from the frequency and the manner in which children share reading with their peers or teacher. In fact, their spontaneity and their growing sense of autonomy can be seen in the way they plan their sharing time. A simple form like the one in figure 5.4 becomes a revealing part of a child's portfolio.

Most children enjoy sharing their reading; many feel that their reading improves as a result of sharing. And most children do get better because they have incentive not only to practice more, but to reflect more on their practice. There will always be children, however, who demand more private engagement. And that is their right—as long as they are comfortable with their choice and the teacher is certain it isn't lack of confidence that inhibits sharing and collaboration.

The Development of Confidence as a Reader

One factor that has tremendous impact on both a child's reading capacity and enjoyment is his confidence in himself as a learner and, specifically, as a reader. Many things can be done to ensure that children become confident in their abilities. And many dimensions of home and school environments all but guarantee that children's confidence will flourish—or flounder.

I begin with a brief discussion of conditions that threaten children's confidence. First, grouping practices that either create or perpetuate stereotypes of "good" and "poor" learners undermine confidence (Braun 1985). As has been noted earlier, such practices place children in situations where chances of success are dictated by personal, social, and instructional factors. These circumstances limit not only the goals that teachers set for low-achieving children, but those that children set for themselves. Grouping influences what

Fig. 5.4 Preparing for Sharing My Reading

Name ______________________________ Date ________________

Name of piece for sharing: ______________________________

Source of piece
- ☐ from library
- ☐ from home
- ☐ my own writing
- ☐ ____________________

How I will go about preparing
- ☐ on my own
- ☐ help from friends
- ☐ help from teacher
- ☐ listening to a tape
- ☐ help from home

How I plan to share
- ☐ make a tape
- ☐ in front of group
- ☐ at home
- ☐ with a partner
- ☐ ____________________

How my sharing went
- ☐ I enjoyed it
- ☐ others enjoyed it
- ☐ it was too long
- ☐ it was too short
- ☐ it was just right
- ☐ it needed extra work
- ☐ ____________________

What others said about my sharing: ______________________________

____

____

____

Notes to myself to help with future sharing: ______________________________

____

____

____

Comments from my teacher: ______________________________

____

____

____

children learn to expect of themselves and the degree of confidence with which they approach school tasks.

Second, undue emphasis on competition channels learning energy in the wrong directions. Children who suspect that they are not progressing according to expectations of teachers and parents are likely to give up and prove over time that they are not powerful learners. This occurs not because of deficiencies in learning capacity but because of a lack of confidence in their abilities, and consequently, in a subsequent decline in effort.

Third, in classrooms where the secrets of learning remain the domain of the teacher, children feel both powerless and helpless—feelings that impede self-confidence. Generally, children in such environments do not understand the bases for their successes or failures and are unable to monitor their continued learning, to fix what needs to be fixed, or build on what can be built on. These children typically have no notion what to attribute their few successes to and may attribute their failures to deficiencies within themselves. They are set up for continuing failure.

What, then, can teachers do to foster self-confidence in learners? First, they must avoid the pitfalls of inappropriate grouping and competition. Second, they must engage in collaborative monitoring. This goes a long way in building confidence. By sharing secrets about children's learning, teachers give children a clear message that whatever problems they face, the problems belong to them. The children know, however, that there is support for them to find solutions to their learning problems. Continuing discussions with peers and teacher help children understand the nature of their learning and discover what kinds of strategies result in what kinds of learning. They gradually get the message not only that the problems are theirs, but so are the solutions. Confidence is the essence of empowerment.

Often children who have already decided that they are poor learners need to be jolted from their perceptions. Jessica is a case in point:

> Jessica, a fifth grader, had all but given up on herself as a learner; in fact, she seemed quite comfortable as a failure. After all, as she herself admitted, "I'm the dumbest in the class." That seemed to her a good enough explanation for her problems. Jessica had developed a classic case of "learned helplessness." If she tried at all, she would try once and then sit back and wait for assistance or direction.
>
> One day her teacher, Keri McKane, decided to invite Jessica to a special conference. She gave Jessica a sheet with the following categories, "Things I do well," and "Things I don't do well." Keri asked Jessica to fill in her form over

> the next two days; Keri would fill one in as well. Then they would get together to share information. Predictably Jessica listed eleven things she didn't do well with not a single response in the positive column. Keri had things in both columns, including such comments as "does the most creative drawing," "does beautiful reading during reader's theater when she has a chance to listen to a tape beforehand," and so on. Jessica's response to each of Keri's comments was "Oh, I didn't know that counted."
>
> That was the beginning of a long but sure trek toward the development of confidence and a growing self-sustaining energy for Jessica. What was required was continuous shared monitoring of her efforts along with work on strategies for improvement.

Keri's work with Jessica points to the need for children to become aware of "where they are" as learners. And this requires that their learning becomes visible to them in an objective way. Telling them they are "good" when they do not see themselves as "good" is not going to persuade them. In fact it may lead to suspicion of the teacher's motives and distrust in her judgment. Children need someone who knows how to get them to look at themselves. Then the stage is set for a symbiosis between advancement in learning and development of self-confidence.

At least one further consideration needs to be highlighted—the importance of listening. Children need to see that their listening abilities have as much status as their reading abilities. They gradually learn to understand that their growing abilities to use language cues to anticipate and confirm meaning during listening, and their growing ability to understand concepts during listening, become the cornerstones of effective reading. Self-confidence, under circumstances in which children are connections between one learning event and a future learning event, has a much better chance of survival, and where it is floundering, a better chance of taking hold.

Concluding Comments

Success in reading depends on many factors. Among these, motivation and confidence are paramount. To a large extent how children feel about learning and the enthusiasm they bring to it depend on the learning environments they create with their teachers. Children thrive on positive learning experiences; they thrive on collaborative rather than competitive engagements.

Long-term learning is built on strategies for learning rather than on an aggregation of isolated skills. Teachers must assess learning environments in their classrooms on an ongoing basis to ensure a climate for healthy growth in attitudes.

Children become fluent readers through continuous engagement with books. It is important at every stage of their development to ensure that they *want* to read and that their strategy development *enables* them to read with ease and enjoyment—children will be unable to read if they won't read. Not only should teachers monitor children's reading, but they must have children monitor their own tastes, interests, and development in reading.

Another aspect to successful reading growth is the development of self-confidence. When children fail to develop as readers, teachers must delve with children into the causes of low confidence, then work with the child to develop self-confidence—the seeds of motivation to continue learning.

REFERENCES

Bialostok, S. *Raising Readers: Helping Your Child to Literacy*. Winnipeg, MB: Peguis Publishers, 1992.

Braun, C. "Teacher Expectations and Instruction." In *International Encyclopedia of Education*, 5008-5001. London, UK: Pergamon Press, 1985.

Braun, C., and P. Goepfert. Strategies. Scarborough, ON: Nelson Canada, 1989.

Landsberg, M. *Reading for the Love of It: Best Books for Young Readers.* Scarborough, ON: Prentice Hall, 1986.

Smith, F. "Learning to Read: The Never-Ending Debate." *Phi Delta Kappan* 73 (6): 432-441 (February 1992).

Observing the Emergent Reader

6

Why Is Observation So Important at This Stage?

There are many reasons for carefully observing all readers. However, there are special reasons why the emergent reader demands the most vigilant perceptive observation. Failure to observe and to provide the best possible environment for the emergent reader carries with it risks of failure and frustration.

Clay (1991) points out that there are many circumstances in the young child's life that can lead to confusion about print. This confusion may have to do with misconceptions about literate behavior generally, as well as expectations about the ways in which readers can and should behave in the act of reading. The confusion may be linked to misconceptions over where to look, what to look for, and how to connect looking, listening, and saying to meaning. Failure to recognize the specific nature of this confusion inevitably leads to inappropriate instruction, and ultimately to the child's persistence in "practising error," as Clay puts it. Whatever interest in reading and writing a child may have had at one time will dwindle and disappear altogether.

Clay warns that the child whose confused learning goes unnoticed will, for a time at least, respond to instruction, but "attends to the wrong features and uses wrong assumptions" (Ibid.: 114). She explains that children who are forced daily to practice errors, to use inefficient strategies, and to build habits of responding on poor foundations are set up for long-term failure. For those who question the need to carefully observe young children, Clay warns: "Six months of muddlement is more than enough to create poor readers of school entrants with average or superior intelligence" (Ibid.: 228).

For Clay, as for others in the nineties, the identification of factors that may cause reading problems lies squarely with the teacher. Reading problems are not to be viewed as deficiencies of the child. She emphasizes that the critical question in the early stages of reading is not so much what the child knows, but "what operations does he carry out and what kinds of operations has he neglected to use?" The need for teacher expertise is highlighted when she says:

> We begin to produce our reading failures by allowing some children to build ineffective strategies which limit what they can do throughout their school careers. As older readers they are difficult to help because they are habituated in their inefficiency and because their processing behaviours are hidden from view. In terms of the computer age they have been poorly programmed. They wrote the program and we do not know how to get into it (Ibid.: 313).

Ways of Looking and Seeing

TAKING NOTE OF LITERACY FOUNDATIONS

Above all else, we must take note of the kinds of learning the child brings to school, the learning that forms the foundations of literacy, including emergent literate activity. These observations form the basis for many of the experiences that are provided for the child at school.

First, does the child bring with him a wealth of experiences—things to talk about, to question, to ponder? These experiences, along with the opportunities he has had to talk about them, form the basis for his ways of thinking about the world and organizing his personal world. Further, from these experiences come the concepts and words that he uses in his own talk. These experiences, on the one hand, originate from his interests, and on the other, spawn new interests.

Second, does the child come to school with a background of book experiences? Does he enjoy stories and seek out new book experiences? Does he have favorite books? Does he volunteer to talk about these? Does he participate as stories are read by predicting, joining in on refrains, and so on? It is also useful to know something about the way a child tells stories, both those he has heard and those that are sparked by his own imagination. Teacher and researcher Karen Clark, on the basis of numerous samples of children's talk, believes that listening to children talk through wordless books provides the richest window to their story experience and their story language. What is relevant to reading is the extent to which children already see the language of ordinary, practical experience and the language of books as contextually distinct, and especially how they are able to reflect experience and stories in connected talk.

It's been a long time since Martin reminded us that rich literary experience is foundational.

> Each of us has a linguistic storehouse into which we deposit patterns for stories and poems and sentences and words. These patterns enter the ear (and the eye) and remain available throughout the course of a lifetime for reading and writing and speaking. The good reader is one who looks at the page of print and begins triggering patterns that have been stored in his linguistic treasury. These patterns range all the way from plot structure...to rhyme scheme...to the placement of an adjective in front of a noun... (1975: 1)

The opportunities for ideas and language to enter into this storehouse vary considerably for children both in and out of school. The school has a responsibility first to determine the kinds of opportunities the child has already had and then to provide a rich abundance of additional opportunities. While many early childhood educators focus almost exclusively on story experience (which is essential) it is equally important to take stock of other literary genres that children bring with them to school such as verse, rhyme, and song. MacLean, Bryant, and Bradley (1987) have established that awareness of rhyme and alliteration that originated from knowledge of nursery rhymes influences later reading and spelling success. The child who brings with him a store of verse and song carries with him material for early experimentation in reading and writing. It is important to note whether or not children have an easy memory for text, and for what kinds of text. Forester and Reinhard (1989) note that children who have wide experience with print often imitate intonation patterns and fluency efforts of expert readers. I have had the opportunity to interact with and closely observe identical twins, Carina and Vanessa. The girls at twenty-three months of age will each pick up a book, go from page to page, and clearly engage in reading-like talk, with rhythms, intonations, and junctures markedly different from those used in their other play activity. These girls have been immersed in the language of singing, chanting, and reading since they were born. Among other things, they already have at least part of the feeling of what it is like to be a reader. The intonations are more than just parrot-like utterances; they respond quite differently as text and illustration change.

To document with one further example, Tyler at seven months has very distinct book preferences. Of course he loves books with illustrations that can be manipulated, but there are times when he demands three or four rereadings of a book with a strong rhythm and flow. These preferences are more than incidental. Tyler is developing a repertoire of language scaffoldings: foundations for language development, generally, and foundations for emergent reading.

Third, it is important to take note of the child's orientation to literacy. To what extent is he aware of the uses of print in everyday dealings—letters, notices, messages, news, and so on? Does he respond in any way to print in his environment—signs in shops or street signs? Does he invent messages, and does he "read" text using his memory of prior readings and illustrations? Does he participate in constructing group stories and poems and in recording important class events? Does he invent tests of favorite stories and take an active role in drama and puppet play activities? Above all, how interested is he in finding new meanings in his environment, through books and everything that surrounds him? That is likely the most critical question of all.

Naturally, children in any class will vary markedly in their background of language and reading experiences. Teachers should not use knowledge gained from observations like the ones referred to above in any sort of diagnostic/prescriptive sense. All children will thrive on extensions of the rich foundational experiences they bring to school. None will suffer from more reading, listening, and talking about and exploring print. Children who have had limited background experiences with story, poetry, or book language of any kind must not be faced with unrealistic expectations about immediate success in learning to read, though. Undue pressure to speed the reading process without providing this rich foundational language experience (which may well involve reading together in appropriately supportive contexts), is likely to result in confusion and frustration. Stewart (1988) goes one step further. He emphasizes the need to look out for the child who suffers the effects of undue pressure and unrealistic expectations to become a reader before he is ready. Such pressures often originate with parents, sometimes with teachers who are concerned about moving children lock-step through a prescribed curriculum. This may result not only in confusion about print but in serious motivational problems. Generally, knowing something about the child's prevailing attitudes about school, and more specifically, about his attitudes toward literacy, can result in action that will prevent reading failure. Such information can certainly shed light on the child who can learn to read but chooses not to. Too bad all teachers of young children don't have access to children half-an-hour before their bedtimes. That might constitute a fairly accurate gauge of the attitudes and practices that make up the home literacy environment.

Hood, watching children in their "group time" activities, observed many indicators of foundational experiences. "They all find the bookshelf, select books, open them and turn pages. Some leaf through before settling on one book. Some curl into cozy spots hugging their selections. Some go through many books quickly... Some read stories aloud... A few still don't hold the book right side up..." Hood finds useful information about children as they sing: "What number will come next as we sing 'This Old Man'?" "Who can read the date on the calendar?" and so on (1989: 29). It is important, as in all observation, that idiosyncratic behaviors are not taken as aberrations but rather as typical day-to-day variations in human attitude, drive, and response.

Liz Stoyko spends a lot of time at the beginning of the school year just talking with children and observing them in talking/reading/listening situations to get a "sense of the foundations." She vividly recalls Sasha who, in the fall, did not participate in any discussions, wandered all over the place while she read to the group, and during some of the class's environmental excursions seemed oblivious to things around him—he certainly displayed no interest in reading signs, or in knowing what information was displayed on posters, and so on. The following journal entry dated September 23 demonstrates sensitivity to the need for taking foundational experiences into account:

> Sasha is just beginning to respond to *some* of the stories and rhymes, especially the ones that are short and snappy. Today he caught himself chanting "Wee Willie Winkie" and was more surprised than I that he was able to repeat the whole, and with a lively lilt. Twice he has volunteered to do the giant's *fee fi fo fum*. Sasha has had no book experience of any sort before he came to school. However, his mother has already been on the telephone twice to see what we are doing in reading. I'm explaining to her as best I can that we are "going slow now in order to go fast" later. She has bought in so far. I'm going to use a lot of the stuff we're learning orally now as Sasha's reading material. It won't be long.

> However, we have to do a lot of work on the oral long after we are into the reading. I'm just going to work the two together.

"Going slow to go fast" is likely a wise maxim to be applied in many classrooms. This does not mean waiting for children to be "ready." On the contrary, it means drenching kids in language and learning experiences, reading to them and with them, talking with them, sharing agenda-setting, writing with them, and generally placing them in a rich literacy environment as together you grow. It takes a perceptive teacher, a good observer, to gauge how much time and energy to devote to what, and how to merge the oral language development with emergent reading experiences. Only day-to-day observation can provide the answers for each child.

BROADENING THE GAZE

In the following section I lay out some of the critical observations needed to ensure that children do not get lost in the "tangles" of confusion without someone being there to help unpick them. More important, I show that perceptive observation prevents many of the tangles from occurring in the first place.

First, children who emerge comfortably as readers have oriented themselves to books appropriately. They are familiar with conventions of title, author, beginning of book, front of book, and so on. They have oriented themselves to hold the book right side up, to start reading on the left page, and so on. They know where to begin on the page, the direction in which the eyes must move along the line of print, and at what point to sweep the eye to the correct spot on the next line.

Second, the emerging reader learns that in many books, meaning comes mainly from print rather than illustration. That is not to say that pictures will not, and should not, be used as clues to understanding print. But the reader must ultimately learn that there is a one-to-one correspondence between words in text and words in speech—each word in text corresponds to a spoken word. Failure of children to understand the relationship among speech/print/meaning is the source of much confusion. This is so particularly when children are expected to make matches at the grapheme/phoneme (sound/symbol) level. An example:

> Aaron knows a good part of the text he is reading by heart: "They all ran after the farmer's wife." He says, "They all ran after..." and comes to a stop—he has forgotten the word *farmer.* His teacher, unaware that Aaron has no sense of one-

> to-one print/voice matching, begins on an exercise frustrating to both (and this is by no means the first). She begins by asking, "What is the first letter in the word *farmer?*" Of course Aaron doesn't know; he is not even sure what a word is. He doesn't know where to look, and even if he did, he has no idea where to look for the "first letter," a concept completely foreign to him. As an aside, Aaron is able to make isolated connections between certain letters and corresponding sounds. Both he and his teacher are hoping that one day "it will all come together."

Such coming together happens in isolated instances in spite of inappropriate instruction, but frustration and failure are much more predictable results. As in learning generally, the development of global concepts and broad relationships precede effective learning of more specific concepts.

I am also reminded of a young adult who had been in school for eight years. He was surprised to find that individual words in speech corresponded to individual words in print. He claimed never to have noticed the white spaces between words in text. Another young adult who had not learned to read by the time he was seventeen thought that his eventual success in learning to read was dependent on his ability to see a word in print and then quickly spell it letter by letter "in my brain." It is just one more example of a child misunderstanding the relationship between print and speech and generally what readers expect of themselves in the process of learning to read.

Clay warns that as long as a "child can't locate a word he is saying in a line of print, he will remain a non-reader" (1991: 1). The need to establish early consistency in directional orientation and a sense of clear one-to-one correspondence is critical. As Clay says, "Although the novice may know only a few words, as long as he controls the movement patterns of one-to-one correspondence, he has created for himself opportunities to learn." The opportunities include talking with others about words and responding to queries from the teacher or others using his knowledge of the critical reference points (words or lines of print). It also allows the young reader to begin making analogies about similarities and differences among words and word parts (Ibid.: 138). This all makes sense, especially when we consider that gross discrimination in learning precedes finer distinction and discrimination.

Third, learners must know that they need to look inside the words for correspondences between letters and sounds to make these finer discriminations. Readers must know how units within written words correspond to units within spoken words—for example, by comparing rhyming elements in words, and noting sound/letter correspondence. How the child views the component parts of written language in relation to oral language can be seen through the writing he does. Too often specific instruction in letter/sound correspondences precedes children's concepts of how the system is supposed to work. The child then develops faulty notions about print, becomes frustrated, and ultimately gives up trying to read.

Finally, there are critical observations to be made when the child moves from "finger/voice pointing" along memorized text to recognition of specific word and letter features relating to word order and overall meaning. Both Clay and Johnston warn that during this transition the less-than-sensitive observer may think that the child is regressing, as the oral rendition of text, for a time, moves away from what sounded like the fluent, natural flow of speech. Clay says that the child has taken a "major step towards integration when his reading slows down and even becomes staccato" (Ibid.: 15). She considers the following as "signs of progress": slow deliberate reading, correct word-by-word reading, increased use of finger pointing, unusual pauses, a more serious attitude, and overt checking and searching. The need to self-monitor to make and to maintain meaning is critical. So is the need to develop strategies to test and confirm alternatives when meaning breaks down. Children must know that they can check and correct error when it occurs. Then they must explore alternatives to develop effective corrective strategies.

The foregoing discussion may suggest that learning to read involves, more than anything, the development of mechanical operations. I hope that is not the case. It is children's general orientation to literacy that is most important. To make meaning of any kind, they must bring their own meaning to text. They must be able to use their knowledge of the language of books to develop fluency as readers.

To reiterate, observing children at the emergent reading stage is most effective in a free and comfortable environment. From the start children need to feel comfortable making "mistakes" and trying alternatives. These alternatives provide teachers with multiple windows into children's thinking about reading. A restrictive environment that undermines confidence and willingness to learn puts bars on those windows and imposes serious limitations on the ways we can help children.

As mentioned earlier, the conditions under which observations are being made determine what we see and hear. On this matter, I take issue with Clay's admonition to achieve objectivity. She warns against the tester's role as a "stimulus to behavior," believing that "all comment, teaching points, helpful replies, leading questions, and pointing guides have to be dispensed with entirely during a reading observation. A guiding maxim is 'Record now; teach later'" (Ibid.: 212).

I find this puzzling for two reasons. First, a testing context is unlikely to uncover the range of behaviors that children typically display in a natural conference or instructional situation. Any constraint on risk taking will mask from our view what is "controlling children's attention." Second, to determine children's zones of proximal development, teaching and prompting and supporting of all sorts are valid. I believe that, first and foremost, observation should help me fine-tune instruction; that is, I have to observe what *I* do (or what a competent peer does) in relation to the competencies of the learner being observed. This allows me to test the results of my instructional choices. In other words observation is an integral part of curriculum and instruction.

Chittenden and Courtney (1989) state that multiple settings for observations allow us to see the unevenness in children's development. Some children react differently to literature when they listen to a story read by the teacher than they do during group reading time—the kinds of questions they raise as they read a book in the group, the kinds of observations they make about characters, and the kinds of links they make with story and everyday events. Some children perform best in unstructured situations whereas others do best in structured contexts. In all fairness, I don't expect that Clay intends observations on the CAP (below) to be interpreted without consideration of ongoing informal observations of a child's behavior. I know that is not the case.

OBSERVATION STRATEGIES FOR EMERGING READERS

➤ Concepts About Print Test (CAP)

CAP is a test devised by Clay as a formal instrument to help teachers check children's concepts about print and books. Concepts explored include knowledge of front of book, place of print and illustration in text, concept of letter and word, first letters, upper- and lower-case letters, and punctuation marks. The test uses the book *Stones*, which features print convention anomalies. The book is read to the child and the child is asked to help the tester by pointing out what is wrong with the book—twenty-four anomalies in all. These include words in wrong order, reversed letters, lines in wrong order, and upside-down pictures. The test, administered individually in about five to ten minutes, has been used in many countries. The best instrument for its purpose, CAP is available in languages other than English, as well as in a version for visually impaired children.

Johnston states that the major limitations of CAP are "error detection" tasks and the fact that the instrument's success at revealing a child's understanding of concepts depends upon the relationship between tester and child. That of course is true in all standardized testing situations. Johnston's point is that the anomalous text may prevent children from responding naturally unless they are completely comfortable. Nonetheless, he claims the instrument is an "excellent record as part of an early screening procedure to locate children who are having difficulty learning these rather arbitrary concepts" (1992: 203).

➤ Observing Knowledge of Print in the Environment

Probably the best way to determine the child's knowledge of print, its functions, and how it is used, is to explore with him print in the world around him. Some of this information will surface through casual day-to-day observations and by listening in on conversations among children. Such observations are especially important with children who come from homes where little or no book activity takes place, with ESL children, and with children from other special populations. We are often surprised to discover that children know as much about print as they do. That makes the effort more than worthwhile.

There are many different ways to facilitate the flow of information about children's knowledge of print. An array of household cartons and labels can be brought into the classroom. This may include cookie carton labels, hot-chocolate containers, candy and gum wrappers, juice cartons, and cereal cartons of all sorts. Labels from household products like toothpaste, soap, and shampoo are useful and may trigger conversation and unexpected comments. As children become responsible for bringing in cartons and labels from home, this exploration of print may have the added result of triggering conversation at home. It will certainly help to raise consciousness of print to a greater degree than an array of neatly displayed adult-designed materials.

Encourage children to talk about the labels. This will uncover their knowledge of item categories, of specific names of products, of the intention behind labels, and of specific words. Probes such as the following help further: "What is this used for?" "How do you know?" "Are there other ways of finding out?" "Can you point to the place where it tells that?" "Why do you think someone put the words there?"

Another way to discover what children know about environmental print is to take them on school and community walks. (A good quality tape recorder or a note pad is useful for recording observations that might otherwise fall between the cracks.) These excursions reveal children's knowledge of signs and slogans—traffic signs, road signs, labels on cars and buses, and so on—and often reveal more insights than weeks of classroom observation. For example, a child who presumably had no concepts of print at all, pointed to the sign that read "Principal's Office," and remarked, "That means be quiet." My grandson, who reportedly had no knowledge of written numbers, one day read the number on a bus passing by: "Oh, that's the *28;* it goes by Ben's house." Nicholas knows numbers when he is interested in them and in real-life contexts where they make sense—a nice starting place to extend instruction and learning. My granddaughter, on a walk one day, stopped by a realty sign and asked, "Where does it say *house?*" Caitlin somehow knew from the shape of sign, configuration of color and symbol, and likely its location, what the sign was for and began to move from the general intent to a more specific query, "Where does it say house?" Interestingly, the word did not appear on the sign, which puzzled her. "Don't they know?" (referring to the realty company) was a logical response for a five-year-old who expects the word *house* to appear on a sign designed to sell a house.

A nice follow-up to environmental walks is a photo display featuring signs and labels found in the child's environment (Braun and Braun 1993). Often, as children talk about these displays, they reveal things that they have had time to reflect on that didn't surface during the walk. All in all, there is much to be learned about children's interests and perceptions from talk about their environment. We miss a wealth of observational information if we don't capitalize on these opportunities.

Often school-based information can be supplemented with information from parents' observations about literacy in the home environment. Parents must be invited to provide this; they don't usually report that kind of information as they don't think it has real value in the overall literacy picture.

➤ Text Assembling: Print Concepts

Text assembling is an activity in which children are asked to take text that has been cut up into individual sentence or word cards and put it back to its original order. Initially this may consist of no more than individual words from a four- to six-line piece of text that the child has memorized. The purposes of this task are to determine to what extent the child is able to reassemble the text, the kinds of self-prompts he uses, and, if he is unsuccessful at certain points during the task, the kinds of peer or teacher prompts that enable him to complete the task successfully. It is an activity that helps the teacher to get a clear sense of many aspects of the child's text knowledge. It is a task that demonstrates both the child's edge of learning and his zone of proximal development. Another advantage to using an assembling task is that it is manipulative, thus inviting movement of text pieces without fear of error. If a word is out of order, it can simply be placed in its right place with the teacher's assistance. And what was wrong can be clearly seen and explained. A task like this invites conversation and is completely non-testlike. It can be repeated with any number of text samples on different occasions as it is instructional as well as observational.

While there are no standardized procedures for text assembling (nor should there be), I outline a sample script here as an illustration (Ibid.).

Read the following verse with the child (or have another more competent reader read the verse with the child). The best advice is to use a piece the child has memorized:

> This old man
> He played one,
> He played knick knack
> On my drum.
>
> With a knick knack paddy whack,
> Give the dog a bone
> This old man came rolling home.

Make a copy of the verse in enlarged print on a large piece of paper or light card, so that individual word cards are about 3 cm by 9 cm in size when later cut up. Make sure the child is comfortable repeating at least most of verse (preferably all of it). ***First, cut the verse into single-line strips***. It is important that the child see the strips being cut up; better still, to have him do it. ***Then scramble the strips and ask the child to reassemble the text.*** (Desk pocket charts are excellent for this purpose.) If the child needs assistance recalling the text, say the first line with him, asking him to locate the strip featuring that line of text. There is no correct procedure; children require varying kinds of assistance as they do in all instructional situations.

Some of the most useful information comes from asking the child strategy questions along the way, such as, "How did you know that line went there?" or "Listen to the word that starts the next line; how can you find it; how do you know it's the right one?"

For children who are having trouble working with text strips, text assembling is a good activity to do with short pieces of text in groups—short group compositions, refrains from fairy tales, songs, and so on. Those who are proficient can proceed to the next stage, assembling the text after the strips have been cut into individual word cards. (Initially, it may be helpful to show the line number of the text on each card, for example, a small #1 on each card in line one.)

Proceed with the word card task in a manner similar to the one outlined above. Give as much assistance as necessary noting the kinds of assistance required. Again, listen for self-prompts.

For children who are having considerable difficulty, consider the following variants of the exercise:

Provide a copy of the complete text and ask the child to assemble the cards as he follows the text (again observing the manner in which he proceeds, for example, letter-by-letter matching, word-by-word matching, unusual hesitations or frustration, and so on). If he has not become frustrated, ask the child to try again without the copy, so you can observe changes in performance.

Observe two or three children assembling an unrehearsed piece. Record their conversation. Then ask them to listen to it with you and to comment on their conversation.

For children who are still having difficulty, use even shorter pieces of text, such as:

Teddy Bear, Teddy Bear
Turn around
Teddy Bear, Teddy Bear
Touch the ground.

Some children find comfort and help in text that has some captioned words as markers:

Bubble gum, bubble gum
BLOW BLOW BLOW
Little bubbles, big bubbles
Watch them GROW

The observations and information that can be derived from this kind of activity are limited only by the teacher's imagination and ingenuity. Text assembling is good because children like to do it, and continue to do it with other texts as they develop new strategies. It is also extremely helpful for determining what strategies less successful older readers employ and discovering where the system appears to be breaking down for them: which print concepts they understand and which concepts reveal sources of confusion. Further, it can be used with ESL children, using text samples from their own language. It is often erroneously assumed that simply because they are unable to read English text, ESL children are non-readers.

You can use figure 6.1, opposite, to record notes from text assembling and other activities.

The use of text assembly tasks has interesting implications for children's "work" at home. And, when children need some extra help at home, it is straightforward enough that parents can assist their children. Sandy Taylor's experience with the task reinforces this notion:

> Sandy had been puzzled by José's slow progress in reading ever since he had entered her class three months earlier. José, seven-and-a-half years old, often memorized pieces of text after having heard them two or three times. Obviously his knowledge of language was not the major impediment to his reading progress. Sandy, who had assumed that José had mastered basic reading concepts, was therefore shocked when she found that as he was "reading" a memorized passage, he had his eyes fixed on the next page—not only had he not mastered word/print matching, he was unable even to match pages.
>
> She then asked José to cut up "Run, run, as fast as you can; You can't catch me..." into individual word cards. José puzzled over the exercise at first. On a second round, however, he showed he understood that the text he had recited from memory earlier is made up of individual words and remarked, "So much words... let me try another one..." Motivated by his discovery, José then took pieces from his folder home so that his older sister could enlarge them and cut them up into cards. Two days later José came to Sandy, pocket chart in hand, with a number of Spanish songs and story refrains that his mother had done

Name ______________________ Date ______________

Child automatically moves from left to right.
Comments: ______________________

Child shows evidence that he/she is able to use some sound/symbol knowledge as cues in locating words.
Comments: ______________________

Child is able to assemble the text with ease.
Comments: ______________________

Child requires assistance to assemble the text.
Comments: ______________________

Child asks for assistance that goes beyond "is this the right word?"
Comments: ______________________

Strategy questions asked by the child: ______________________

Responses of child to strategy probes and prompts (e.g., "How did you know that was right?" "What can you do to find out?" "Do you know other words that start the same, look the same?")
Comments: ______________________

Continued

Fig. 6.1 Observation/Conference Record Form—Text Assembly Task—Continued

General Observations About the Child's Responding

(Include child's perception of his/her own performance. Note any changes in responding as the child becomes more familiar with the task. Make special note of the child's persistence level, tolerance for error, and tendencies to make wild guesses.)

Comments: ______________________________

____

____

____

____

____

Comments from other professionals who have observed the child: ______________

____

____

____

____

Comments from parents: ______________________________

____

____

____

____

Instructional Plans

Child's perceptions and plans: ______________________________

____

____

____

Teacher's plans for strategies: ______________________________

____

____

____

Suggestions for home reading: ______________________________

____

____

____

with him—refrains that reinforced the same speech/print relationships that José had discovered with the English pieces he had worked with in class. For José, this simple task of reassembling text opened up a world of words and ideas. Sandy's response: "How could I be so blind? And how is it that some problems have such simple solutions once you look in the right places?" Two months later, "José has taken off; there is no stopping him."

➤ Target Word Spotting: Print Concepts

I have worked for many years with so-called "remedial" children (around ages seven and eight), who are referred to me for special "testing" and instructional help. What Vernon (1957), and later Downing (1970, 1971), called "cognitive confusion," has accounted for the large majority of these referrals—referrals that might not have been necessary if appropriate observation and instruction had taken place. I feel it is critical to find out about children's concepts of print early on. The price in frustration and emotional stress and the missed opportunities to "get at" text are too great to ignore. And talk encouraged through text assembling reveals children's knowledge of those concepts.

Another activity closely linked to text assembling is target word spotting. This can be done in a small group or individually (Braun and Braun 1993). Children have before them a series of short pieces of text the child should know by heart, such as "Old MacDonald Had a Farm." The teacher reads the line slowly, asking the child to follow with his eyes and finger on his copy. When working with a child individually, after the initial reading, the teacher can simply ask him to point to a specific word. In a small group, children can circle this target word. (In spite of the bad press that paper-and-pencil tasks have had recently, and I am in agreement generally, having a record for discussion is useful in this case.) The circling activity is a prompt to the discussion that follows. The scenario below highlights the kinds of observations that can ensue:

> When Haida's teacher read the first line of "Old MacDonald Had a Farm" and asked the children to circle *farm*, Haida circled the first *I* in the refrain *E-I-E-I-O*. But she seemed perplexed about her choice. During the discussion that followed, the teacher asked Haida to explain why she had chosen the letter *I*. Haida demonstrated by pointing in staccato fashion to individual words as she read. Although she gave three taps to the word *MacDonald*, she assigned a word to each tap (thus getting two words ahead of herself). She knew something was wrong, but didn't know how to go about solving the puzzle.

Haida had just recently discovered that words in print exist as discrete entities, and that these words can be matched to words she assigns in speech as she follows the line of print. This new learning was followed so quickly with yet *another* discovery—some words have more than one syllable—that she was centered on her most recent learning. Normally she would have circled *farm;* now as she focused on the three syllables in the word *MacDonald* she moved her finger and voice to circle the *I*. What to the untuned observer appears to be confusion in fact often marks a new learning point. The teacher learned much about her children, mostly from the discussion that was triggered by the exercise. She was particularly impressed that Haida was able to hear the "parts" in *MacDonald*.

➤ Looking Inside Words: Print Concepts Fine-tuned

Some children take a while to grasp the concept of sound/symbol relationships within the word even after they understand the notion of matching the printed word to the spoken word. Often the child is taught specific relational elements among spoken word parts in text long before he understands how the sound/symbol relational system works. Undetected, that can become a source of confusion and frustration. The following activities can reveal important concepts about the relationships between sounds and print (Ibid.). They can be used individually or in small groups. My preference is for small groups, as children trigger interesting discussion points for one another in this type of situation. Here is an example:

The teacher provides children with a handout of the following verse and writes it on the board:

Little Jack Horner
Sat in a __orner.

The teacher says: "I will read aloud the little verse you have before you. Follow along with your eyes and fingers. Put your finger on the word *corner*. I have left out the first letter in *corner*. See if you can think of the letter you need to fill in the space." (There is no need to agonize over the right or wrong wording for directions. Simply help children till they understand what it is they are expected to do.) For some children it may be helpful to have a number of alternative letters available, such as *n, c, r, t, w,* and ask them to select one that they think will fit.

Again, the discussion that follows is as instructive as the letters that the children select. They will reveal their theories about what fits and what doesn't fit, though they may not always know why. A sampling of responses from children might include: "I know that one; it is the same as Corrie's name"; "I said it over and over to myself and listened to the start of my lips"; "I have the verse at home, and I looked at it."

A similar task involves concept of rhyme in print (Ibid.). Children are provided with selections like the following:

A woodpecker pecked a little round hole
Right on top of the telephone p_____.

After the text has been read by the teacher children are asked to provide the ending for the target word. Again, children must understand what the exercise is about. And it may be necessary to read the verse a number of times inviting children to join in the reading. The observations that come from this kind of exercise vary greatly. Some children will consciously use the *ole* from *hole* to write *pole*. Others will listen to themselves and write their own version, like *pl*, *pol*, or other variants. What will be uncovered is whether or not children are able to apply their knowledge of rhyme in speech to make rhyme analogies in print, and more generally, whether they can use knowledge from one part of text and apply it to another. What will be observable is the degree to which they actually practice what they know—but this practice depends on their ability to listen to themselves. Again, their own comments are often the most valuable observations that derive from such activities.

The exercises that have been described here provide useful information if children are allowed to do them in groups of three or four. The kinds of strategies children use and the notions they have about what are effective often manifest themselves in different ways when they know there is no expert around to bale them out. Not only do observations in these situations provide excellent instructional guidance for teachers, they provide a good way to let children and their parents know that they are moving along in productive ways.

Children working in pairs or small groups have a remarkable way of cuing each other, making comments that prompt and probe the thinking of their peers. Having a peer make a wrong response often triggers an alternate response from another. From my own observations, when children are left to their own resources, their responses often reveal more "I know this because..." and "It must be ________ because..." than when there is the likelihood of adult intervention.

I hope that the suggestions I have made here are not seen as an endorsement of fragmenting the reading process. Their purpose is to observe children's knowledge of more specific concepts in relation to the more global concepts that have been discussed earlier in the chapter. Again, for many children, these day-to-day observations of their work with text will reveal this information.

It helps to organize conference notes to use as benchmarks against which instruction can be gauged. These notes become part of the semi-permanent record but can be shared with other professionals about particular children if and when the need arises. Categories like the following can be used to document the observations:

- Child selects (circles, fills in) spontaneously
- Child shows evidence of particular strategy use in responding
- Child benefits from assistance and prompts
- Child shows evidence that he/she knows when an inappropriate or questionable response has been made, or demonstrates confidence in knowing when a response is on target
- Hints for instruction/follow-up observation suggested by the exercise

➤ Mini-Cloze Exercises

As both Clay (1991) and Johnston (1992) have suggested, a child's writing provides a good record of his concepts about print. This includes not only his growing knowledge about how the system works, but also knowledge of specific sound/symbol relationships. The most useful information, of course, is derived from observation of children's writing in a wide range of contexts. Children's inventions and concepts of print conventions always form an essential part of their learning record. Mini-cloze exercises also serve well as both observational and instructional/learning prompts. My personal preference is to select a piece of verse that children already know by heart, and then to give them copies with key letters deleted. For example:

Original piece	*Cloze sample*
I saw, I saw, I saw	**I _aw, I _aw, I _aw**
A lion at the zoo.	**A _ion at the _oo.**
I saw, I saw, I saw	**I _aw, I _aw, I _aw**
A baby tiger, too.	**A _aby _iger, _oo.**
I saw, I saw, I saw	**I _aw, I _aw, I _aw**
A great big kangaroo.	**A __reat _ig _angaroo.**
I saw, I saw, I saw	**I _aw, I _aw, I _aw**
I saw them at the zoo.	**I _aw _ _ em _t the _oo.**

(Braun 1985: 47)

This exercise invites a great range of possibilities and can be used in a number of ways. Different letters can be deleted. Children find it an interesting way to show what they know. Some, like Sandy, who commented, "I didn't even know that I could do that," discover new insights about their abilities and their learning. The day after completing a cloze test, Sandy asked for another piece "the same as yesterday—just a different verse." The second day, the teacher observed that Sandy listened to herself much more closely than she had the day before.

In the same class there were a few children who were not ready to tackle the exercise independently; they were given other options. Some were paired with a more able peer; others asked if they could look at the teacher's copy when they needed to, an excellent strategy. Todd, after one of these sessions, made the comment, "I say the word, I look at it real carefully, then I listen to myself over and over again just like Michael does."

Very often, after a few tries with support from others or after referring to the teacher's copy, children suggest that they can write the whole piece without any help. In a sense this exercise, initially at least, is a self-dictation activity with prompts.

Mini-cloze exercises are considered by some as the antithesis of invented spelling. If these exercises were imposed on children who did not already grasp global print concepts, I would agree. However, when used with children for whom the "big ideas" are already in place, and who have long engaged in their own inventions, these exercises reveal much. They show children hearing themselves say words and developing perceptions of the specific links between specific sounds and letters—links we expect to develop.

➤ Other Strategies

Another observation strategy is to listen to children read orally to get a sense of how they are processing text and to see how well they self-monitor their reading. Miscue analysis and running records are the most common of these practices.

For a detailed discussion and analysis of miscue analysis refer to *Reading Miscue Inventory: Alternative Procedures* by Goodman, Watson, and Burke.

Since their use applies more to mature readers than to emergent readers, I discuss running records in the next chapter.

EARLY SUCCESS: CONFIDENCE AND STRATEGY

The need for the development of confidence was discussed in the previous chapter. However, the issue is particularly critical at the emergent reading stages. Feelings of success are paramount if natural growth is to take place—children are confident as long as they feel they are in control. They need to attribute successes to their ability to draw on existing strategies and to develop new ones. That means that they have to be able to monitor their own learning and talk with the teacher and others about their learning. With their teacher they can then plan how to extend and apply existing strategies and how to develop new ones.

I must offer a word of warning. Confidence in doing the wrong things well is no more productive for children than it is for teachers. In the long term, a false sense of confidence that has developed from reliance on ineffective, narrow strategies is unlikely to result in effective reading. Harris (1976) warned us many years ago of the negative consequences that come from a lack of flexibility in reading tasks and purposes. For example, Clay warns that it may be counterproductive to perceive reading as the learning of an aggregation of sound/symbol associations rather than as a process by which the reader develops the types of strategies that enable him to extend his own learning and "self-improve." She emphasizes that a child's reliance on a narrow range of learning through wrong program emphasis may result in a lack of flexibility. Since this is so closely tied to what we choose to observe, I quote from Clay:

> **Our enthusiasms act like blinkers: they give us tunnel vision. We select our course, measure what is important, and give practice to habituate those skills we value. Any programme can become counter-productive if children are**

> helped to habituate only a narrow repertoire of reading behaviours, no matter how effectively we teach (1991: 240).

Still, there is a need to observe and record any impediments to the child's confidence. Sometimes as children observe others in the room who have developed more independence than they have, they feel threatened—especially when peers, parents, even teachers, make comments like "James is just pretend reading." James is in fact emerging in healthy ways as a reader. "He just memorized it" is another common criticism. Even the most subtle suggestions of competition can challenge reader's confidence. The best antidote is sharing and developing peer support systems, systems of cooperation and learning together.

The best insurance for successful reading experiences is to experiment with the child to find the zones of comfort and challenge—zones that provide comfort when he is working independently and challenge when support is readily available. The exercises in this chapter can be used along with any number of day-to-day observations to guarantee successful reading. It is a matter of finding out the interest levels of the children, knowing what materials to give them, then providing the kinds of prompts/supports they need at the moment they move toward independence on a given strategy.

TEACHER REFLECTION ON OBSERVING EMERGENT READERS

Since observation of the emergent reader is tied so intimately to his successes, I want to discuss some of the changes teachers experience in relation to their observation of young learners. In the last decade, based on new research and information, our assumptions about how children learn have changed dramatically. This new knowledge can be applied to teachers too, when we view *them* as learners.

Neilsen says that "while we often talk about differentiated curriculum and instruction for younger learners, we tend to act as though teachers, as learners, are 'all grown up' and all the same." He notes that differences in personal needs and preferences among adults suggest varying strategies to promote change and growth. There is a danger that frenzies of "change talk", coupled with one-shot professional development sessions, often lead to superficial, cosmetic change accompanied by a "false sense that change has occurred" (1991: 7). These change facades or masquerades are often brought on by external pressure to change, and result in little more than what Neilsen calls "procedural compliance with administrative and/or curricular directives."

True change in observation and instruction has to come from beliefs about children and learning. These changes are then both reinforced by, and modified through, continued observation and instruction. That is the foundation for significant change, and it can happen only when the climate is right. Teachers need to reflect on, talk about, and write about what they have observed. They need to be free to take risks. As mentioned earlier, teachers as learners need to be in control of their learning. They need to feel free from competition that accompanies external testing of their students and concerns of how the results compare with others across the system or country.

A good example of cooperative, reflective learning comes from a small-group sharing meeting. Four first-grade teachers and a resource teacher got together to share notes on two children who appeared to be "stuck" as readers. The two teachers whose children were having problems brought extensive notes on what they had observed. In addition, they brought a few tapes of children's attempts at unrehearsed reading. After about forty-five minutes, one of the two teachers exclaimed, "I'm just looking at pieces, in fact, very small pieces—not even the most important pieces." That comment turned the whole discussion to the importance of looking at the global concepts children bring to learning. The revelation of one teacher inspired her colleagues to think about their own observations of children and teaching practices. The meeting ended with plans to go back and observe these children further, to find background reading on child development in relation to learning (specifically emergent literacy), and to meet again two weeks later to continue discussion. At the next meeting, all five decided to bring in observations of children that related to their initial discussion. After two-and-a-half months of meetings, the following observations were made by members of the group, three of whom by this time were connected by electronic mail:

> *My gaze has broadened, and it is continuing to broaden, sometimes in the most unexpected ways. For one thing, I am just beginning to understand the difference between children's development of associations and the development of strategic control over their learning. I can't believe how that changes what I do in the classroom! I can't believe how that changes what I see and hear!*

> *Sherry* [one of the initial target children] *is going like a house on fire. Most of the time I forget that she ever had problems. To think that I could have been responsible for her failure. Just scary!*

> *I have changed a number of things; I am also hanging on to many of the things I did before. Only now I am beginning to understand why I'm doing them; also when not to do them with certain children. You're never too old. I'm sure proof.*

Substantive change often occurs with little fanfare, and seldom needs to be accompanied by new language to describe the changes. In fact buzzwords and slogans, apart from the fact that they tend to disguise real change, often lead to a bandwagon mentality. Those who don't blindly buy in may feel intimidated and marginalized. Teachers willing to self-reflect and share their beliefs with others, and to employ a little ingenuity to solve problems, hold the key elements to change.

Some teachers find a self-assessment form like the one in figure 6.2 (page 134) a good place to start their own questioning and reflection. The statements, a reflection of my own focus, will hopefully change as teachers reflect on their learning and move forward in their observation strategies.

Honest stock taking when filling in a form like figure 6.2 raises many questions—questions that can become excellent triggers for teacher discussion and professional development sessions. Relating the statements to actual practice can stimulate much reflection and talk. For example, the third statement, "I emphasize global concepts and understanding..." is a generalization that likely has more potential applications in learning and instruction than any of us will ever realize. It therefore warrants continued examination and reflection. The generalization stands as a reminder of the need for children to understand the whole so that they have connecting points for new learning—learning related to that whole. To translate the concept into practice is an ongoing concern. Sharing the insights and questions raised on these forms can stimulate teacher network discussions.

Concluding Comments

With emergent readers we must use observation to discover the foundations of literacy that they bring with them to school. This means observing them in as many situations as possible and opening dialogues with parents to broaden our gaze.

We must continually broaden this gaze as we observe children. Only then can we be sure that we are providing them with the best possible learning environment. Observation can be restricted by narrow assumptions about

Fig. 6.2 Examining My Assumptions About Emergent Reader Observation

Name ______________________ Date ______________

	Yes	*Need To Think About It*	*No*
I am aware of the impact of hidden curriculum agendas.	☐	☐	☐
On examination, I am aware of some of my own proneness to hidden agendas.	☐	☐	☐
I emphasize global concepts and understanding before I examine the presence of more specific concepts (e.g., basic print concepts before letter knowledge and specific sound/symbol relationships are emphasized); I continue to work at discovering all that this generalization means in emergent reading generally.	☐	☐	☐
I am working at discovering children's zones and tying observation and instruction to that knowledge.	☐	☐	☐
I am expanding the breadth of indicators I use to evaluate children's reading development.	☐	☐	☐
I understand the need to observe children's development in listening and writing in relation to their reading.	☐	☐	☐
I involve children at all levels of the assessment process.	☐	☐	☐
I am on constant vigil for impediments to self-confidence.	☐	☐	☐
I take note of any impediments to the development of flexible reading strategies.	☐	☐	☐
I am more and more aware of the difference between limiting effects of associative learning of isolated items and long-term power of learning of self-extending strategies.	☐	☐	☐
I am looking for more and more subtle indicators of children's motivation to explore reading on their own and for subtle indicators of an expanding range of purposes they see for reading.	☐	☐	☐

	Yes	*Need To Think About It*	*No*
I am growing in my ability to take risks, and I strive to foster risk taking in my children.	☐	☐	☐
I am aware of the need for children to develop fluency strategies, and give high priority in instruction to meet that need.	☐	☐	☐
My classroom is a rich literacy environment that allows observation of the widest possible concepts about literacy.	☐	☐	☐
I invite suggestions from colleagues and parents to enable me to observe children from diverse language and social backgrounds to avoid marginalizing them through unfair, limiting observations.	☐	☐	☐
Other ______________________________	☐	☐	☐
Other ______________________________	☐	☐	☐

Reminders: ______________________________

learning, limiting literacy environments, and a climate that inhibits risk taking by both teacher and children.

Many strategies can be used to stimulate children's learning; from these we get observational data that informs appropriate instruction. It is especially important to ensure that some overall global concepts about knowledge of how written language works are in place before children are subjected to instruction in the more specific aspects of reading. These concepts include knowledge of the relationship between oral and written language generally as a prerequisite to learning more specific one-to-one links at the sentence, word, and sound/symbol levels. Failure to do so has long-term implications, perhaps of failure as a reader. As we listen to children talk about print in their environment we glean vital information that can be supplemented by more structured approaches.

When observing emergent readers, it is imperative at all stages to ensure a climate that promotes self-confidence. This confidence is essential for a child to take risks and to develop flexible reading strategies—to attempt new strategies when others fail. The slightest threats to self-confidence should be noted and talked about with the child, and if necessary, with parents.

Self-reflection by the teacher is as important as observation of children—it is the basis for ongoing change. Many teachers have achieved tremendous growth in their observational and instructional skills and in self-confidence through discussion of assessment and learning issues with supportive colleagues. Both self-observation and observation of the emergent reader are key to teachers' development of successful learning environments. ESL and other "high risk" children are prone to marginalization unless competent, open, professional observation is available for them.

REFERENCES

Braun, C., and W. Braun. *Early Reading Profile.* Calgary, AB: Braun and Braun Educational Enterprises, 1993.

Braun, W. "A Teacher Talks to Parents." In *Breaking Ground: Teachers Relate Reading and Writing in the Elementary School.* Edited by J. Hansen, T. Newkirk, and D. Graves. Portsmouth, NH: Heinemann, 1985.

Chittenden, E., and R. Courtney. "Assessment of Young Children's Reading: Documentation As an Alternative to Testing." In *Emerging Literacy: Young Children Learn to Read and Write,* 107-120. Edited by D. S. Strickland and L. M. Morrow. Newark, DE: International Reading Association, 1989.

Clay, M. M. *Becoming Literate: The Construction of Inner Control.* Portsmouth, NH: Heinemann, 1991.

Downing, J. "Children's Concept of Language in Learning to Read." *Educational Research* 12 (1970): 106-112.

Forester, A. D., and M. Reinhard. *The Learners' Way.* Winnipeg, MB: Peguis Publishers, 1989.

Goodman, Y. M., D. J. Watson, and C. L. Burke. *Reading Miscue Inventory: Alternative Procedures.* New York: Richard C. Owen, 1987.

Harris, T. L. "Reading Flexibility: A Neglected Aspect of Reading Instruction." In *New Horizons in Reading,* 331-340. Edited by J. Merritt. Newark, DE: International Reading Association, 1976.

Hood, W. J. "If the Teacher Comes Over, Pretend It's a Telescope." In *The Whole Language Evaluation Book,* 27-44. Edited by Goodman, Goodman, and Hood. Portsmouth, NH: Heinemann, 1984.

Johnston, P. H. *Constructive Evaluation of Literate Activity.* New York: Longman, 1992.

MacLean, M., P. Bryant, and L. Bradley. "Rhymes and Nursery Rhymes and Reading in Early Childhood." *Merrill Palmer Quarterly,* 33 (3): 255-282 (1987).

Martin, B., and P. Brogan. "Teaching Suggestions for Sounds Jubilee." In *Towards a Reading-Writing Classroom,* 1. Edited by A. Butler and J. Turbill. Portsmouth, NH: Heinemann, 1987.

Neilsen, A. R. "Examining the Forces Against Change: Fulfilling the Promise of Professional Development." *Reflections on Canadian Literacy* 9 (2): 76-88, (1991).

Vernon. M. D. *Backwardness in Reading.* London: Cambridge University Press, 1957.

Observing Children's Oral Reading

7

Teachers and Children Listen to Oral Reading: Errors as Windows

There is no specific point in the development of young readers where we can say they are no longer emergent readers—as long as they are learning, readers are constantly emerging in new ways. The discussion in this chapter does have relevance for children we normally consider emergent readers but for the most part extends to readers who have developed more mature reading strategies. We must remind ourselves, however, that many children at age seven or eight are emergent readers in the truest sense.

Using children's oral reading as windows to their thinking about reading and the kinds of thinking they do as they read originates with Goodman (1969, 1970) and Clay (1982, 1985). Ken Goodman refers to his system of listening to, recording, and interpreting oral reading as *miscue analysis.* Marie Clay refers to *running records.* The systems have the potential for similar observations and interpretation. Both use the determination of patterns of errors or *miscues* as a basis for inferences about the child's reading processes. They differ essentially in the mechanics of recording. For purposes of this chapter I limit myself to a detailed discussion of running records drawing extensively on Clay (1985) and Johnston (1992).[1]

[1] The section on running records in the Johnston book has been written in collaboration with Marie Clay.

USING RUNNING RECORDS

The mechanics of drawing oral reading samples by conducting running records involves three pieces of equipment—a piece of text, a piece of paper, and a pen (tape recorders are optional). As the child reads, the teacher uses a special shorthand system to jot down what he is reading on a blank piece of paper. (See pages 141–146.)

Johnston sees a number of advantages to using running records over other systems of recording. First, the system is flexible and requires a minimum of fuss with materials and preparation. Second, the procedure is unobtrusive. The child does not feel that he is being tested, especially if he is assured that he can see what the teacher has recorded (something that makes good sense anyway). This means that the procedure can take place often, yielding many samples of reading at different times, based on a variety of materials.

Using a tape recorder is a matter of individual style and preference. Certainly taped renditions of oral reading provide excellent sources for practicing the mechanics of running records. I use the recorder extensively as a means of having children listen to their own reading. It also provides a record for me to listen to when I haven't time for one-on-one reading and listening/recording.

There are a number of other advantages too. Tapes allow me to listen to a child's reading of the same piece a number of times to determine what changes occur as he listens to himself and tries again. The ongoing record provides the teacher with a source of information to use for instructional guidance as well as information to explain and defend the curriculum. The tapes and records can be extremely valuable parts of a child's portfolio—showing child, teacher, and parent the kinds of changes that have taken place. So are the child's accompanying reflections on what he perceives caused the changes in reading over time. This attribution of successes to personal decisions (made in collaboration with the teacher) is one of the best assurances that constructive learning will continue.

Tapes should be well organized. Careful labeling, with attention to name, date, footage, and accurate referencing of materials, is essential. Otherwise the system will break down immediately. Charts used to record this information may become a permanent part of a portfolio, a reading log, or a "reading fun folder."

The following section describes in detail the actual process of recording information. The system, devised by Marie Clay, has become well known as part of her Reading Recovery Program.

Coding Words Read Correctly

As the child reads, the teacher records each exact representation from text with a check mark. This is shown in the child's reading of the following piece of text:

Text:

One day Buster Bear became very sleepy.
It was time for a long winter's nap.

Child reads:

One day Buster Bear became very sleepy.
It was time for a long winter's nap.

Running record:

✓ ✓ ✓ ✓ ✓ ✓ ✓
✓ ✓ ✓ ✓ ✓ ✓ ✓ ✓

It is simply a matter of making one check mark for each word read correctly, lining up the pattern of check marks to correspond with the pattern of words in text. The coding becomes more complicated as the reader omits words from the text, as is shown in the next sample.

Coding Omitted Words

Text:

There was a little turtle
Who lived in a box.
He swam in a puddle,
He climbed on the rocks.

Child reads:

There was a turtle
Who lived in a box.
He swam in a puddle,
He climbed on rocks.

On-the-spot record:

✓	✓	✓	—	✓
✓	✓	✓	✓	✓
✓	✓	✓	✓	✓
✓	✓	✓	—	✓

Final record:

✓	✓	✓	— little	✓
✓	✓	✓	✓	✓
✓	✓	✓	✓	✓
✓	✓	✓	— the	✓

Note that a dash is used to represent each word missed. The omitted word is later recorded below the dash.

Coding Substituted Words

Text: The winds tossed the craft up and down. Clearly, they were lost.

Child reads:

The storm tossed the boat up and down. Clearly, they were lost.

Running record:

✓ storm/winds ✓ ✓ boat/craft ✓ ✓ ✓ ✓
✓ ✓ ✓

In this example, the word the child substituted is recorded *above* the dash. It is important to note that while the reader has substituted his own words for some of the author's, meaning has been maintained.

Coding Self-Corrections

Unlike the substitutions noted in the running record above, readers often find that a word doesn't make sense given the overall sense of the text, or the words immediately surrounding the miscue. These corrections are coded using the letters *SC*, for "self-corrected." The word read originally is recorded along with the word in text.

Text:

One day Nicholas found something shiny at the entrance to the ice cave. He stopped short and called to his cousin, Caitlin.

Child reads:

One day Nicholas found something shinny at the entrance of the ice cave. He stopped short and call to his cousin, Caitlin.

Running record:

✓ ✓ ✓ ✓ ✓ shinny/shiny | SC ✓ ✓
✓ to/of | SC ✓ ✓ ✓ ✓ ✓ ✓ ✓
call/Called | SC ✓ ✓ ✓ ✓

The reader of the passage above made a quick judgment, and decided that *shinny* wasn't a word that made sense to him given what had preceded or followed in the text. The word *call* was blurted out quickly, but just as quickly changed; it simply did not fit syntactically with the overall tense of the piece, and did not parallel the tense of the word *stopped*.

The extent to which readers make self-corrections and the kinds of corrections they make are extremely important indicators of how they think about text and the strategies they have available to solve text problems. They predict and monitor on the basis of their semantic knowledge and on the basis of what makes sense syntactically. In concert with this they use their sound/symbol knowledge to make sense. In all this, of course, their experience with the particular genre of the text and situational context involving authors' intentions and readers' expectations determine the kinds of self-corrections readers make. For example, readers approach text organized in different ways with varying expectations and varying strategies corresponding to those expectations. Lists, menus, and so on are read with different expectations and intentions than narrative. The rhythm of a limerick triggers different expectations and strategies than a report on pet care (Harste 1984; Watson 1988).

While self-correcting generally is regarded as a highly positive strategy, if practiced to the extreme it becomes a liability to fluency. Johnston (1992) cautions that too much concern on the part of the reader over self-correcting, especially over trivial errors that make little difference to overall meaning, becomes disruptive and impedes the flow of reading. And, he cautions, self-corrections are not always made audibly. Nonetheless observing a child's processes of self-correction is one of the best ways to gain information that has an instructional payoff. As well, a report on the child's move to more efficient self-correction should be shared with both the child and parents. That kind of report has greater value than many other things we do for the sake of accountability.

One of the chief purposes of noting self-corrections is to determine the kinds of strategies the child employs to solve text problems. For that reason careful records of these corrections must be kept and compared over time. It is also important to note corrections that result from a child's language background. Children whose first language is not English, for example, may correct on the basis of syntactic overlays from the other language. Certainly variations in pronunciation are to be expected and should not be viewed as evidence of a reading problem. These observations are important, as the main objective of the exercise is to find out about the child's reading strategies; reasonable interpretation is possible only against the background of language and social information about the learner. When in doubt about a child's background, get the information firsthand: ask the child and consult the parents.

Coding Inserted Words

Whenever children add words to the text, these words are coded the way that substituted words were coded in the sample earlier. To indicate that there is no matching word in text, a dash is shown underneath the inserted word, as in the following:

Text:

Solomon Grundy
Born on Monday.
Christened on Tuesday,
Married on Wednesday.
Took ill on Thursday...

Child reads:

Solomon Grundy
Born on Monday.
Was christened on Tuesday,
Married on Wednesday.
He took ill on Thursday...

Running record:

✓ ✓
✓ ✓ ✓
was/– ✓ ✓ ✓
✓ ✓ ✓
He/– ✓ ✓ ✓ ✓

Coding Repetitions

For various reasons, many readers—fluent and non-fluent—repeat words. Often this behavior is a nervous reaction and can become a habit. Or it may be that the reader is trying to prove to himself or others that he "can do better than that." At other times it may simply be that a repetition is a way of gaining momentum with a segment of text, a way of enhancing fluency.

To code repetitions, the letter *R* is recorded next to the check mark representing the repeated word. A superscript (for example, R^2, R^3, and so on) is used to indicate the number if there is more than one repetition. The repetition of a larger segment of text is indicated with the letter *R* beside a line that returns to the beginning of the repeated segment.

Text:

Once upon a time there was an ugly old troll
who lived deep in the dark woods. One day the
ugly troll met the strangest animal...

Child reads:

Once upon a time there was an ugly old troll
Once upon a time
who lived lived deep in the dark woods. One day the
ugly troll met the strangest strangest strangest animal...

Running record:

✓ ✓ ✓ ✓ R ✓ ✓ ✓ ✓ ✓ ✓
✓ ✓ R ✓ ✓ ✓ ✓ ✓ ✓ ✓ ✓
✓ ✓ ✓ ✓ ✓ R^2 ✓

Used to excess, repetitions do get in the way of fluent, efficient reading. It is important then, to determine the underlying cause of these repetitions and to work with the child to overcome the problem.

➤ Additional Information

To achieve the most complete picture of the child's reading, it is helpful to include some additional notes to complement the running records. For example, a child may not attempt certain words. He may ask for help, which can be coded in the following manner:

—/CH *during reading;* $\frac{—}{\text{text word}}\Big|\frac{CH}{T}$ *after reading*

The *CH* indicates the child called for help; the *T* indicates that the teacher told the child the unknown word. As for giving prompts and probes for unknown words, my preference is to test the effectiveness of a range of useful prompts and probes throughout daily instruction rather than to include this information as part of the running record.

Johnston (1992) also includes indicators of fluency, a category I regard as very important. These indicators are: fluent (F), finger-pointing (FP) where the child points word by word during reading, voice-pointing (VP) where the child doesn't use his finger but clearly separates each word as though he were using his finger, and dysfluent (D).

➤ Making Sense of Information from Running Records

It is one thing to learn the technique of coding readers' responses through the use of running records. Unless there is a system to organize this information for easy access and interpretation, however, the exercise is useless. Though everyone has his or her own way of doing this, I offer a few suggestions for organizing information to provide easy access, interpretation, and reporting.

Devising a system for recording an individual child's errors/miscues is the first consideration. A useful form is shown in figure 7.1. The following running record transcript and accompanying sample show how this would be used.

The Wolf and the Seven Kids

Once there was a mother goat who had seven little kids. One day, she called to her kids. "I have to go out to look for food," she said, "Do not open the door while I'm away or the wolf will come in and eat you up."

"How shall we know the wolf if he comes?" asked the seven little kids.

"You'll know him by his gruff voice and his black feet," said their mother. "Now be good." And off she went into the forest.

Soon there was a knock at the door. A voice called, "I'm home, my dear children. Open the door so that I can come in." But the seven little kids said, "You are not our mother. You have a gruff, growly voice. You are the wolf."

The wolf went away and ate a piece of chalk. This made his voice soft...

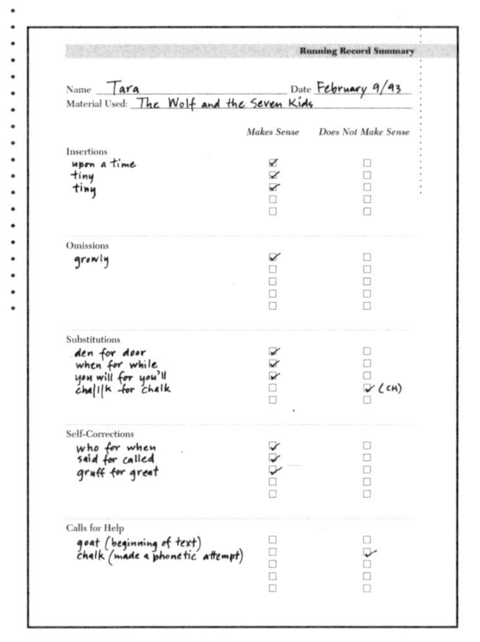

Running Record Summary

Name: Tara Date: February 9/93
Material Used: The Wolf and the Seven Kids

	Makes Sense	Does Not Make Sense
Insertions		
upon a time	☑	☐
tiny	☑	☐
tiny	☑	☐
	☐	☐
	☐	☐
Omissions		
growly	☑	☐
	☐	☐
	☐	☐
	☐	☐
	☐	☐
Substitutions		
den for door	☑	☐
when for while	☑	☐
you will for you'll	☑	☐
cha/l/k for chalk	☐	☑ (CH)
	☐	☐
Self-Corrections		
who for when	☑	☐
said for called	☑	☐
gruff for great	☑	☐
	☐	☐
	☐	☐
Calls for Help		
goat (beginning of text)	☐	☐
chalk (made a phonetic attempt)	☐	☑
	☐	☐
	☐	☐
	☐	☐

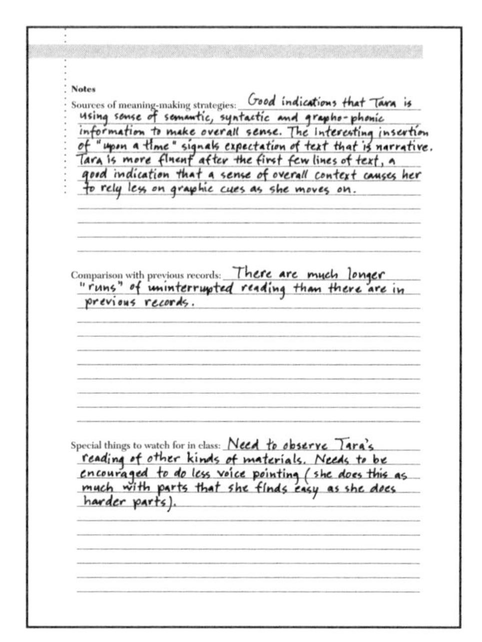

Notes

Sources of meaning-making strategies: Good indications that Tara is using sense of semantic, syntactic and grapho-phonic information to make overall sense. The interesting insertion of "upon a time" signals expectation of text that is narrative. Tara is more fluent after the first few lines of text, a good indication that a sense of overall context causes her to rely less on graphic cues as she moves on.

Comparison with previous records: There are much longer "runs" of uninterrupted reading than there are in previous records.

Special things to watch for in class: Need to observe Tara's reading of other kinds of materials. Needs to be encouraged to do less voice pointing (she does this as much with parts that she finds easy as she does harder parts).

Running Record Summary for *The Wolf and the Seven Kids*

I have omitted repetitions, partly to make the form more manageable, but also because the categories listed in the form appear to have the greatest impact on meaning-producing strategies. It is important, however, to make notes regarding children's lack of attention to specific graphic and phonemic features in the "special things to watch for" section. Note evidence of over-reliance on these features, to the point where meaning is lost or fluency is impeded. Further, if running records are used to determine suitable reading material for the child, the notes should include evidence of what would be appropriate; for example, use of material more familiar to the child, more predictable, or with a rhythm that might enhance reading. An ongoing record of the kinds of text that each child finds easy or hard is useful to have. That information is helpful in the short term for selection of materials, and in the long term for designing instruction that will enable the child to use an increasing range of strategies and to apply these strategies easily to more challenging materials.

Some teachers choose to record periodic reading rates (number of words read per unit of time) as they take running records, as well as accuracy rates (proportion of correct to misread words). If this practice is followed, note the potential pitfalls. First, number of words read may fluctuate widely from one kind of material to another and from one time to another. Purpose of reading

Name ______________________ Date ____________

Material Used: ______________________________

	Makes Sense	*Does Not Make Sense*
Insertions	☐	☐
	☐	☐
	☐	☐
	☐	☐
	☐	☐
Omissions	☐	☐
	☐	☐
	☐	☐
	☐	☐
	☐	☐
Substitutions	☐	☐
	☐	☐
	☐	☐
	☐	☐
	☐	☐
Self-Corrections	☐	☐
	☐	☐
	☐	☐
	☐	☐
	☐	☐
Calls for Help	☐	☐
	☐	☐
	☐	☐
	☐	☐
	☐	☐

Continued

Fig. 7.1 Running Record Summary—Continued

Notes

Sources of meaning-making strategies: ____________________

Comparison with previous records: ____________________

Special things to watch for in class: ____________________

will also influence rate. Regarding accuracy rates, I like to think that listening to a child's reading, along with a general description (as in figure 7.1), provides all the information necessary. Reliance on numerical information suggests more precision than running records warrant, an artificial measure that can mask a process that requires subjective judgment—finely-tuned professional interpretation. However, it may be helpful, especially for older children, to see visible evidence of progress in these areas. That can justify some quantification as long as learners see how open to error such a process is. Teachers, however, need to realize the variability that may result from the kinds of situational/contextual circumstances that influence performance during test-taking. In the case of younger emergent readers, we should heed Clay's reminder that some children slow down or exhibit staccato-like reading while they are integrating new learning.

For accessibility, it is a good idea to place running records in a loose-leaf notebook. Use at least ten blank forms for each child and tab each child's form with his or her name to ensure easy access during teacher and child review and parent interviews.

➤ Children's Self-Analysis of Running Records

Having children both record and analyze their own performance is another excellent way to use running record data. For this to be successful, however, the child must be given an opportunity to discuss his previous running records with the teacher—he needs to understand clearly the intent of the records as well as the procedures. It is also important that teacher and child listen to and discuss running record performance during interview/conference time.

With that kind of background there is no reason why children cannot begin to do their own short records. They should start by taping very short selections. They do not need to code the information the way we do. Further, the number of categories for analysis is likely best kept down to two: "makes sense," and "does not make sense." Too many demands may confuse and discourage them. All they need initially is a form like the one shown in figure 7.2 (page 153).

A teacher's typical first reaction to this exercise is "my kids could never do that." My response: "Of course they can't, unless someone teaches them how." And it's not easy; it takes time. However, by the time children have a good sense of the process involved in responding, the reflection that has gone on has already resulted in major improvements in their reading strategies. Sometimes, in fact, it is a good idea to have two or three children work cooperatively. Keep track of the arguments of what "makes sense" and what "does not make sense" based on their discussions. Eventually, introduce a third category—"makes some sense." What becomes clear, in spite of what appears to be confusion, is that children gradually become expert monitors of their own reading. They can talk about their abilities, areas that require additional practice, or strategies that need to be developed.

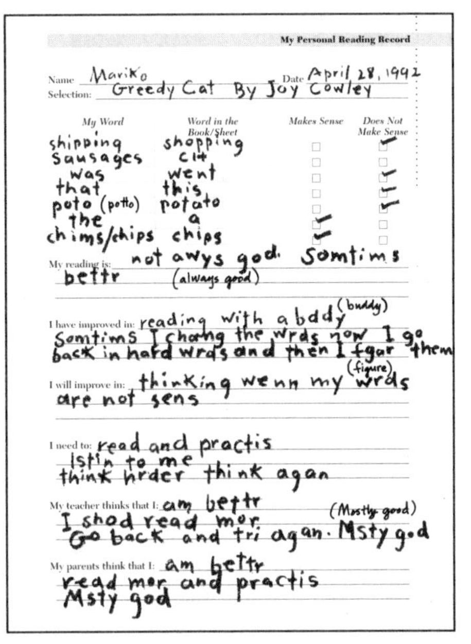

My Personal Reading Record

Name: Mariko Date: April 28, 1992
Selection: Greedy Cat By Joy Cowley

My Word	Word in the Book/Sheet	Makes Sense	Does Not Make Sense
shipping	shopping	☐	✓
sausages	cit	☐	☐
was	went	☐	✓
that	this	☐	✓
poto (potto)	potato	☐	✓
the	a	✓	☐
chims/chips	chips	✓	☐

My reading is: not awys god. Somtims bettr (always good)

I have improved in: reading with a bdd (buddy) Somtims I chang the wrds now I go back in hard wrds and then I fgar (figure) them

I will improve in: thinking wenn my wrds are not sens

I need to: read and practis lstin to me think hrder think agan

My teacher thinks that I: am bettr I shod read mor Go back and tri agan. Msty god (Mostly good)

My parents think that I: am bettr read mor and practis Msty god

Sample of completed Personal Reading Record

It is both interesting and helpful to have children review and compare with you your record in relation to their own records. Then talk about the improvements that have taken place and reflect on *why* both of you think the changes have occurred. Added benefits frequently come when teachers discuss freely with kids the specific changes they make in their instruction as a result of discussing these records. For example, children like to know, first that teachers are ongoing learners, and second, that the information they have provided has been useful for teacher learning.

Such is the case with Karimm, a third grader, as he talks with his teacher about his records from October to February. The discussion goes like this:

Karimm: [looking at his earlier forms] *I read so many "no sense" words. Now there are so few.*

Teacher: *Why do you think that is?*

Karimm: *Well, I think more when I read words... like what it will be about, and... I sometimes just keep on going.*

Teacher: *How does that help you?*

Karimm: *Well, I think... does this fit, or what word goes here? I sometimes quickly go back and change a "no sense" word.*

Name ______________________ Date ______________

Selection: ______________________________

My Word	*Word in the Book/Sheet*	*Makes Sense*	*Does Not Make Sense*
		☐	☐
		☐	☐
		☐	☐
		☐	☐
		☐	☐
		☐	☐
		☐	☐

My reading is: ______________________________

I have improved in: ______________________________

I will improve in: ______________________________

I need to: ______________________________

My teacher thinks that I: ______________________________

My parents think that I: ______________________________

Fig. 7.3 Reading Process Observations

Name ______________________ Date ______________

Selection: ______________________________

Word in the Book/Sheet	*Word Read*	*Makes Sense* tried to correct	*Makes Sense* did not try	*Does Not Make Sense* did not attempt	*Does Not Make Sense* correct attempt	*Does Not Make Sense* incorrect attempt
		☐	☐	☐	☐	☐
		☐	☐	☐	☐	☐
		☐	☐	☐	☐	☐
		☐	☐	☐	☐	☐
		☐	☐	☐	☐	☐
		☐	☐	☐	☐	☐
		☐	☐	☐	☐	☐
		☐	☐	☐	☐	☐
		☐	☐	☐	☐	☐
		☐	☐	☐	☐	☐
		☐	☐	☐	☐	☐
		☐	☐	☐	☐	☐
		☐	☐	☐	☐	☐

Comments: ______________________________

Strategies to highlight: ______________________________

Teacher: *Remember we talked about these things earlier? And you and I made a list of things you could do to improve?*

Karimm: *Yes.*

Teacher: *Well, these things worked, didn't they? Remember, I made some suggestions and you made some—but you made them work for you. I am going to talk with Theresa and Jack about some of the same things. I have learned something from you.*

Karimm: *Oh, neat...*

Once teachers and children are comfortable with recording information in the manner shown in figure 7.2, page 153, add categories such as "tried to correct" and "did not try" under the general heading of "Makes Sense." Under "Does Not Make Sense" the following could be included: "did not attempt," "correct attempt," and "incorrect attempt." Figure 7.3, Reading Process Observations, opposite, illustrates how this might look.

➤ Using Running Records to Analyze Teacher Practice

On the matter of teacher learning, the continuing running records provide essential information to fine-tune instruction for individual children. To expand on the discussion in chapter four on teacher change, these records can provide an excellent mirror for the teacher as both learner and teacher. What is required, however, is periodic examination of running records from the whole class taken over a period of time. The following describes how this may happen:

> Frank Youstis, a third-grade teacher, has been using running records for the past year, mainly for the lowest achieving readers in the class (a total of nine children). He is very pleased with the way individual children have progressed since he started using the system in conjunction with other observation practices. Five of the nine children have become expert self-monitors, capable of recording their own reading. Further, they have shown remarkable insights into the adjustments they must make to become even better readers.
>
> Recently Mr. Youstis did a detailed study of errors his children had made over the last three months. This was partly triggered by his realization that even some of the good readers in class had made a greater number of nonsensical intrusions in their reading than usual. The first thing that he noticed was the inconsistency with which at least three children in the "running record" group

read. Sometimes they made few or no nonsensical "errors"; at other times, many. He took action. First, he compared the materials that seemed to create the problems with those materials that didn't. Then he drew some tentative conclusions. To test his ideas, he placed materials of each kind on a large table and asked the group of nine to discuss them. They confirmed at least one of his hypotheses: one set of materials was much more interesting than the other. Words such as *boring* and *stale* were used to describe one set. Words such as *interesting, neat,* and *awesome* were used to describe the other. Mr. Youstis also discerned differences in writing style between the original materials. The materials that had caused problems contained a lot of short, staccato-type sentences, that often left the reader confused about connections between sentence-to-sentence ideas. In retrospect, it was easy to see how the children's predictive, monitoring, and confirming processes might be impeded rather than facilitated with these samples. For the most part, the opposite held for the material the children found easier. It consisted of well-formed text that demonstrated the natural rhythms of language. Mr. Youstis explains:

> "I knew all about the problems for reading and writing when poorly formed text is used for children. I had just never thought of the problems in relation to either facilitative or impeding effects on the actual reading process. I guess the whole notion was there in a kind of theoretical cloud. I thought the notion was great, but had never really given serious thought to any applications in my classroom, except, of course, that I try to make quality literature available to the children. And deep down I felt that some of the 'easy' materials with more repetition of words made more sense to kids who were having difficulty. Now I realize—those kids are exactly the ones that need quality materials most. I am learning; I hope not too late. Of course, I should not have to be reminded that children, even children who are having problems, need to have greater choice in what they read. The problems should never have occurred. I have learned!"

The vignette shows how summarizing observational information (including running record data) can effect individual teacher beliefs and practice. Even the slightest adjustments can make a big difference. As Mr. Youstis said, "I don't think that my discovery will result in a revolution in my teaching, except I can see where I need to look over my observations of the whole class from time to time to see the bigger picture. For a few of the nine kids this one observation has made a dramatic difference in their reading and their writing —in the level of interest. I guess for these kids it is a revolution. Well, in that case it is a revolution in my teaching." This confirms what we have known for so long—that materials can limit or facilitate reading proficiency (and create expectations about reading in children that are counterproductive).

Exercises in examining class learning and teaching often come from global questions about learning and instruction; often they lead to additional questions such as:

➤ Am I promoting and demonstrating reading strategies that focus above all else on meaning?

➤ Are materials conducive to the development and application of meaning-making strategies?

➤ Do I promote flexibility in use of strategies according to the type of material and purpose for reading?

➤ As part of this flexibility do I help children develop and apply specific graphophonemic strategies in concert with syntactic, semantic, and pragmatic knowledge?

➤ Do I engage children in helping me uncover their capacities and needs, as well as the characteristics of my instruction?

➤ Do I discuss with colleagues, including other professionals, teaching concerns that emerge from observations?

➤ Using Running Records Collaboratively

The aspect of discussion with other professionals is often shortchanged. At times the teacher may feel threatened by the involvement of outside professionals. This often leads to a climate of competition, or at best, cordial tolerance. In the best interest of the child, these feelings must be set aside. It has proven helpful, especially in cases of serious learning difficulty, to have teacher and resource teacher (or psychologist) independently conduct a series of running records and then share their findings. That often leads not only to critical clues to the child's problems but to a new level of professional communication and trust. Further, it gives added credence to the message communicated to both parent and child.

Running records then can yield a wealth of information that is useful for both accountability and instruction. Further, they provide a collaborative focus between teachers and children, among peers, and among professionals and parents.

I earlier mentioned the need to put together information from all possible sources to arrive at a composite picture of the reader. With that recommendation goes a word of caution. There may be a tendency in some instances to use running records in too prescriptive a manner. For example, a teacher has decided that a child inserts words; therefore he needs a particular kind of instructional help to overcome the problem. The decision has been made without looking at the total picture derived from the running records. The example points out a misuse of running records that is based on a blatant oversimplification of the reading process. Marie Clay gives frequent examples of what competent readers do. These help us maintain a broad perspective when interpreting data from sources like running records. Following are some of the "strategies for problem-solving new words" that Clay says competent readers use:

- They make an estimate supported by the text.
- They search for relevant information to resolve conflicts among competing responses, selecting those that help to make sense ("a tutorial highlight in which they are instructing themselves").
- They choose enough information to solve a problem.
- They derive unknown words by analogy.
- They partially sound the words and complete the solution by using meaning.

Opinion varies about the place of meaning and sounding in the overall problem-solving process, but Clay's list is one of the more useful ones to generate thought and provide a broad perspective. And perspective is what is needed to make any system work; that is what is needed to ensure productive, ongoing learning of both children and teachers.

Teachers and Children Listen to Oral Reading: Assorted Approaches

There are many other situations, natural and controlled, that provide opportunities for children and teachers to listen to the quality of oral reading. In some of the examples shown here, the insights one obtains about the processes children use in reading will be byproducts of activities designed for completely different purposes. In other cases the purpose will be to stage situations to get a closer look.

ASSESSING FLUENCY THROUGH VERSE

Many children learn to read well enough to satisfy the demands and expectations of home and school through the first few years of school. They develop strategies that enable them to read simple text without considerable support. Many of these children become frustrated as soon as expectations (their own, and those from home and school) to read more text and more complex text overwhelm them. A pervasive problem is that many of these children have never developed the fluency to read a piece with ease and confidence.

Children develop reading strategies as they read materials at a wide range of difficulty levels. However, the ability to use these strategies fluently and automatically requires that they spend a great deal of time reading materials that they find easy. For some the problem may be that their listening repertoire, especially of predictable, easy-to-memorize pieces, is limited. Many children find comfort in revisiting pieces from their earlier listening repertoires and pleasure in discovering that they are able to read these with fluency and confidence. Encouraging children to spend much time reading and rereading pieces that are easy for them all but guarantees that they will develop fluency. Such materials include pieces in which the rhythm of language helps to propel the reader, as in verse, poetry, songs, and refrains. Many of the better known fairy tales and fables are useful as well, especially if children are thoroughly familiar with the genre. Of course many shared and supportive reading experiences also facilitate the development of fluency.

The following strategies have been found to be helpful in checking children's fluency.

First, I involve children in reading (either individually or together) different types of text. I look for both text with natural language rhythms and contrasting text that is stilted and unnatural. I use the following piece as an example of natural rhythm text. It features both sweeping phrases like "Can't you stop and play a bit," as well as the staccato-type "Hip, hip, hip."

Come hippopotamus,
HIP, HIP, HIP!
What an ugly face you've got,
What an ugly lip.

Can't you stop and play a bit?
Dance and hop and skip?
Come hippopotamus,
HIP, HIP, HIP!

Individual children or a group can read the verse aloud (it can be transferred to an overhead transparency if a group is involved). It should be read through a number of times (with teacher's help if necessary), recorded, and then discussed. Are children able to hear differences between the way they read the longer phrases and the ways in which they read the *hip, hip, hips*? While they may not have adult language to talk about their reading, the point of interest is first, do they read the parts distinctly differently, and second, do they hear the differences?

Or have the children read a poem or verse consisting of sweeping phrases such as parts of Ezra Jack Keats's *Over in the Meadow*. After they have read and recorded one or two stanzas of the natural-language text a number of times (and listened to the best reading) have children read and tape a piece like the following, which consists of wooden, unnatural phrasing:

Pat sat on the mat.
Nat sat on the mat.
Pat has a hat.
Nat has a hat.
Pat and Nat sit on the mat.
Pat and Nat have a hat.
Do they sit on the mat?
Do they have a hat?

Ask children to talk about the reading of each and decide which sounds best, how they felt as they read each piece, and the differences or similarities in how they read. To your surprise, you may find some children who in fact like their reading of the second sample better than the first. As one child said, "It sounds just like we read at school." The sad fact was that it did. Equally sad, some of the material used in the classroom invited exactly that kind of staccato-like non-rhythmic response.

Another fluency exercise involves using a number of versions of verse that have the same basic rhythmic scaffolding. For example, the following two verses have a similar overall beat to "Wee Willie Winkie":

Little Tony Tolliver
Went to school.
Learned his lessons quickly
No more fool!

Went up to the teacher
Grabbed her chalk and stick.
Little Tony Tolliver,
What a lunatic!

Little Tilly Tompkins
Lost her teeth.
Got them stuck
In a slab of beef.

Took them for a fix-it job
As soon as necessary.
Slipped into the dentist's chair
To find a kind tooth fairy.

Children practice reading the "Tony Tolliver" piece, then record it and listen to themselves. Then they read the "Tilly Tompkins" version for comparison. Often children who have listened to themselves do much better on the second piece than they did on the first. That is useful information for the teacher; that is useful information for children as they aim to learn more and more about the nature of text and about the characteristics of their own reading.

Sometimes children benefit from having curved lines marked over natural language clusters (phrases) that let them see that certain parts in text are clustered. For example:

Come hippopotamus,
HIP, HIP, HIP!
What an ugly face you've got

This is especially helpful if they can see and hear an expert reader at the same time, and then try themselves.

So far the discussion on fluency has dealt with what appear to be surface problems; they are not. Many fluency problems are closely linked with the child's expectations about reading and what reading aloud should sound like. Many fluency problems stem from some children's lack of awareness of the sounds of their own reading. The exercises mentioned above are attempts to both solve these problems and to develop awareness about the sound and feel of expert fluency. Figure 7.4, opposite, is an example of a self-assessment form that has been useful in helping children listen to themselves and critique their own fluency levels (Braun and Goepfert 1989: 171).

A lack of fluency is often a symptom of an inability to determine the appropriate balance of cues—semantic, syntactic, and graphophonemic—and to apply these cues in determining a word. Further, some children have problems with many high-frequency words so are unable to deal fluently with text even if they know what to do and what it's all supposed to feel and sound like. A problem with individual words, of course, will be noted as part of the running records information. And solving that problem is critical.

It is useful for teachers to look at how their instruction influences the factors that develop fluency. Figure 7.5, page 164, provides a checklist of statements that might appear on a teacher's assessment agenda.

While the foregoing section has addressed fluency assessment, the natural spillover into learning and instruction is striking. And that, of course, is what happens as teachers observe and change instruction based on their observations. The same results occur in reader's theater.

ASSESSING FLUENCY THROUGH READER'S THEATER

Involvement in something as enjoyable and engaging as reader's theater helps children who are disenchanted with reading lose their self-consciousness about reading and focus on the creation of a performance. Many perform in ways they or their teachers thought impossible. (In a sense that is also true of the use of verse.) Reader's theater is so different from the kinds of materials children associate with assessment that they often forget about their anxieties and fears. Children often see activities such as reader's theater as a chance at new beginnings. It is something they haven't tried before; it is something they haven't failed at before. Apart from the optimism often engendered by a new setting and new experiences, an activity such as reader's theater has the potential to disclose surprises about children's abilities that they have not been able to reveal in other more constrained reading settings.

There is no formula for selecting materials for reader's theater. The best materials generally are the those that are scripted by teacher and children. (Competent first- and second-grade children can produce excellent scripts and learn a tremendous amount about both reading and writing in the process.) In selecting stories for scripting, it is good to start with short pieces.

Name ______________________________ Date ______________

Selection: ____

How I Read	*First Time*	*Second Time*	*Third Time*	*Fourth Time*
My reading was smooth and interesting.	☐	☐	☐	☐
My reading was mostly smooth and parts were interesting.	☐	☐	☐	☐
My reading was quite bumpy and not very interesting.	☐	☐	☐	☐

Comments: ____

____

____

____

____

____

____

I can make my reading smoother and more interesting if I ______________

____

____

____

____

____

____

____

____

____

Fig. 7.5 Instructional Practices to Promote Fluency

	Yes	*Mostly*	*Needs Thought*
I recognize the development of fluency as an absolute prerequisite for enjoyment and ongoing engagement in reading.	☐	☐	☐
Materials for instruction invite fluent reading naturally.	☐	☐	☐
I recognize the need to develop critical listening as an aid to fluency.	☐	☐	☐
I am aware of the need for lots of practice with easy material as a necessary means of developing fluency.	☐	☐	☐
I make instructional provisions for children whose word reading is inefficient.	☐	☐	☐
I am conscious of the fact that pressures and nervousness get in the way of fluency.	☐	☐	☐
I model fluency many times every day.	☐	☐	☐
I avoid having children exposed to bad oral reading.	☐	☐	☐
I have available a wide variety of interesting books, including some at very comfortable reading levels.	☐	☐	☐
I encourage children to revisit books they have listened to being read earlier.	☐	☐	☐

Instructional adjustments and questions: ______________________________

____

____

____

Some of the retold fairy tales like "The Three Bears" or "Hansel and Gretel" are excellent. With very young children, of course, the teacher will do the scripting—and the teacher may well decide to include fairly extensive parts for the narrator, a part that she will likely read, at least initially. Just about any poem that children enjoy also provides good material for scripting. Initially, however, it is best to select poems that have parts for a person or animal to speak. In pieces like this scripting involves no more than deciding who is going to read which parts. A simple poem like Margaret Wise Brown's "Little Black Bug" is a good place to start. The piece could be scripted something like this:

1st reader: **Little black bug,**
Little black bug,
Where have you been?

2nd reader: **I've been under the rug.**

3rd reader: **Said little black bug.**

1st reader: **Bug-ug-ug-ug.**

Observe children reading their parts without previous exposure, then after they've had the opportunity to rehearse a few times. Have the reading taped so that the children are able to react to their own readings—talk about what changes they have made from one reading to another and what further changes they would expect of themselves in subsequent readings. This also provides an occasion for children to comment positively on the reading of their peers.

Traditional tales, fables, virtually any short story that lends itself to dialogue, also make good reader's theater material. Following is an excerpt from "The Ghost of the One Black Eye" by Carole Spray (Braun and Goepfert 1989). It has high interest potential and invites readers of various levels to demonstrate what they are able to do. It also allows readers to demonstrate their progress after practice and assistance.

With this script, children can show what they are able to do with varying degrees of support. As they listen to their reading they note in the margin what they want to change on the next reading. (Younger children can simply tell the teacher what they propose to change.) The teacher can then see not only what children's perceptions are of their own reading, but whether or not they have the strategies to make the adjustments they propose. The interplay between sound and sense allows the teacher to see a child's interpretation of character as well as fluency improvements. Through their intonations, expressions, and so on, it likely provides the best window possible to detect whether or not children appreciate the subtleties of irony, sarcasm, and humor in text.

The Ghost of the One Black Eye

		Reader Notes
Narrator:	*A family was sitting around the kitchen table one morning, when the baby started to cry.*	
Baby:	*Waa...waaaa! I want my apple juice. Waaa...!*	
Big Sister:	*Don't cry, baby,*	
Narrator:	*Said the baby's big sister.*	
Big Sister:	*I'll get you some juice. It's down in the cellar.*	
Narrator:	*So the big sister went down the cellar steps, and when she got to the bottom, she heard a deep voice say,*	
Voice:	*I AM THE GHOST OF THE ONE BLACK EYE!*	

ASSESSING PHONEMIC STRATEGIES THROUGH POETRY CLOZE

It has long been recognized that children's writing is one of the best indicators of their sense of sound in relation to print. Not only does their writing manifest their ability to use specific phonemic strategies, it reveals much about their concepts about print. Johnston mentions the power of dictation tests for reflecting children's phonemic awareness and their ability to "represent phonemes alphabetically" (1992: 352). In extensive work with young children I have found that writing of either a self-dictated piece (something children know by heart) or a piece dictated by someone else reveals much about their sound/symbol sense. What is more, I have found that these exercises often help children to "see" what they know.

Simple poetry cloze works well; children frequently volunteer to do more. Children are provided with copies of the poem, with letters missing. The teacher reads the original intact version of the poem at a pace that allows the children to fill in the deletions comfortably. It is best to start with a piece that children know by heart—this requires less attention to what the teacher (or other person dictating) is saying, as they are able to anticipate what follows. The alternative is to have a recorded piece for them to listen to. This allows them to try a part, stop the tape, work on different parts, moving back and forth at their own speed. It frees them from the embarrassment of slowing others down; it also relieves them of the pressure that comes from knowing that the teacher (when dictating) has other work that is waiting. Another approach is to have children dictate to each other.

The following cloze piece is an example that might be used initially. Children are simply asked to fill in the missing letters as someone dictates the intact text to them.

Whisky Frisky

Original piece	*Cloze sample*
Whisky, Frisky,	Whisky, __risky,
Hippity, hop.	Hippity, __op.
Up he goes	Up he __oes
To the tree top.	To the __ree __op.
Whirly, twirly,	Whirly, __wirly,
Round and round.	__ound and __ound.
Down he scampers	__own he scampers
To the ground.	__o the __round.
Furly, curly,	Furly, __urly,
What a tail.	What a __ail.
Tall as a feather,	Tall as a __eather,
Broad as a sail.	__road as a __ail.
Where is his supper?	Where is his __upper?
In the shell.	In the __ __ell.
Snappy, cracky,	__nappy, __racky,
Out it fell.	Out it __ell.

Depending on the child, the teacher can delete as few or as many letters in the piece as necessary to get the information desired. For example, do children hear the sounds in words? Are they able to represent these sounds with letters that approximate those sounds?

There are alternatives to the approach. Children who are reluctant to do the task can be given a copy of the original intact text, as well as the cloze text. The observation then becomes one of seeing to what extent the child needs to use the copy, and for how long. Some children match letter by letter; others take a quick look and that is all that is necessary for them to complete a word. Some find that after they have done one or two pieces with an intact copy they have the confidence and ability to move out on their own.

Another useful approach is to have two or three children work together to complete the task. The conversation (and arguing) reveal both to children and teacher information that would otherwise be hidden.

The following scenario from a first-grade classroom illustrates the potential of poetry cloze:

> I handed out copies of an eight-line verse to the children for them to fill in. There were four versions—the first with the text intact, the second with a few vowels missing, the third with the same vowels plus some beginning consonants missing, the final version with at least half of the letters missing. They were to work their way through versions one to four. The children were not familiar with the text "Mix a Pancake" so we spent five minutes chanting the piece together. Then I let them loose, although the teacher had warned me that most of the children were not capable of doing the task. The teacher and I circulated as the children began working quietly. At first some children were confused about the exercise. But as we encouraged them to say the verse out loud and to listen to the parts missing in each word (I even encouraged some to feel their lips as they were saying the parts), the class started to sound like a beehive. Children moved ahead with the exercise much to their own surprise and to the greater surprise of the teacher. Some looked back and forth to the original copy (a few with an obvious sense of guilt); others listened to themselves intently. It wasn't long before Kari approached me with the most enthusiastic "I'm finished. Can I write it on the back without any of the letters to help me?" She did, and before long, so did others.
>
> Most of this particular session was spent observing what the children were capable of finding out about themselves as learners. Kari put it best: "Mrs. Neill always says listen to yourself; she is right, it really helps." Jakie, a somewhat more cautious learner who was just beginning to feel comfortable with the Eng-

lish language, said, "I take home. My sister help," and this without prompting from anyone. Jakie was able to see that the activity was worth his investment in time and energy.

Exercises like this allow children the freedom to progress at their own pace; they can see how successful they are and where they need help; further, they realize that listening to the sounds of words has big payoffs. Such exercises promote listening to the order of sounds in words and representing these with corresponding letters. They reinforce in many ways concepts about print they are applying to reading and provide visible evidence of their learning, an ultimate boost to confidence.

ASSESSING SENSE OF TEXT THROUGH TEXT TALKS

Much information about children's reading and listening can be revealed by talking with them about text, either individually or in groups. Much observational information comes from children's response to listening to text. (Much of their knowledge about text comes from listening to text, as so much of the sense of text is tied in with pitch, stress, juncture—features that have to exist in children's minds as natural echoes of speech.) In the past, we have assumed much about children's reading knowledge without observing what they do and think as they listen to text when someone reads text to them or with them. We now know that many assumed reading difficulties in fact revealed children's inability to understand text, generally, rather than reading problems, per se.

The exercises outlined here combine both reading and listening. In the first example, children are provided with one or two stanzas of text:

One day I saw a downy duck,
With feathers on its back.
I said, "Good morning, Downy Duck,"
And it said, "Quack, quack, quack."

One day I saw a curly dog,
I met him with a bow.
I said, "Good morning, Curly Dog,"
And he said, "Bow-wow-wow."

When the children have a good sense of the rhythm and content, they together compose their own stanzas based on the rhythmic structures of the original. (That sense can only come about from reading together, and listening to themselves and each other.) They might be given a prompt like, "One day I met a scarlet bird." Then they would have to decide on the "givens" in the stanza. One group of children did the exercise this way:

> "Let's listen to the second line in the first two stanzas again." Some of the children were visibly beating the rhythm (a good clue to what they were attending to). One child said, "We need to say something about the scarlet bird or something like that." Another child said, "Let's decide what the scarlet bird will say in the last line, and then we'll find something to rhyme at the end of the second line.

The discussion disclosed much about their knowledge of the structure of text —rhythm, rhyme, sense, and so on. Their final version went like this:

> **One day I met a scarlet bird,**
> **He woke me from my sleep.**
> **I said, "Good morning, Scarlet Bird,"**
> **And he said, "Tweet, tweet, tweet."**

Another group came up with this version:

> **One day I met silly skunk,**
> **It looked as if it hurt.**
> **I said, "Good morning, Silly Skunk,"**
> **He replied, "Squirt, squirt."**

Other types of text can be used as well. For example, the sample text about spiders, opposite, is used to illustrate "text talk." The whole exercise can be conducted orally. My preference is to combine the oral and visual by putting material like that illustrated on transparency and working through the text. With individual children or groups of two or three, you can use the computer screen in the same way, by scrolling up new information.

The discussion continues as you gradually expose each piece of text. This kind of discussion should be used with brief sections of narrative and never be continued to the point where the children become bored. It can also be extended to children's own writing, especially writing that has reached the revision stage. It is often helpful to leave a piece for a few days (long enough to have forgotten specific details of a piece) and then to read individually or in groups as parts of the piece are progressively exposed. Such an exercise reveals much about children's knowledge of text, especially about connectives and other devices that give cohesion to text. Instructionally it raises children's awareness of text cues that remind them (as readers and listeners) of what has happened earlier, and what to anticipate. Children thus become increasingly aware of how they can help readers "think back" and "think ahead" as they revise their own pieces of text for readers.

Text Talk About Spiders

Text	*Discussion*
The spider is one of nature's most peculiar creatures.	What do you think the author is going to write about? How do you expect her to go about the piece? Why do you think she starts out like this?
[Expose next section of text] First, ...	What do you expect the author to tell you now? Why do you suppose she used the word, "first"?
[Expose next section] it manufactures its own home...	How close were we to the general idea?
Not only is this web the spider's home, it also...	What do you think the author is going to write about next?

ASSESSING READING/LISTENING THROUGH RETELLINGS

Retellings have become popular as ways of finding windows to children's reading and sense of text. Retellings—a child tells a piece of text back in his own words—give a sense of how much of the content a child (as reader or listener) can recall. Even more important, retellings provide a picture of the child's ability to use text features that give form to the text. These features include settings; words used to mark new episodes, like *then, all of a sudden, before long;* and the order of text—from setting, to events, to resolution. In prose, we want to determine children's awareness of words that hint at text organization (structure)—*as a result of, because, therefore,* and so on. Naturally, words used to connect ideas and to signal structure links in narrative and rhetorical features in prose are not mutually exclusive. Often children demonstrate a good sense of the text as a whole (i.e., showing this by ordering and connecting events). This often frees them from recalling exact details from text and allows them to supply their own. As long as these details make overall sense they are to be valued as important to the retelling.

Certainly retellings provide a means to show what children consider important in text. I have known many children (and adults), referred to as "reading problems," who thought they had to recall every bit of information, preferably verbatim. Boontan, a low-achieving fourth grader, illustrates the point:

> Boontan was referred to the Reading/Language Clinic because he wasn't "making any progress in reading." On one of his first visits to the clinic the student clinician and Boontan read together an old tale, "Too Much Noise." When Boontan was asked to retell the story in his own words, he made every attempt to recall exact words from text, interrupting himself every few words with "Don't know anymore." The student clinician's prompts and probes were of no use to Boontan, as he was unable to recall verbatim words from text. Intensive follow-up talks (actually many conferences) revealed that Boontan thought that good reading was a process involving the memorization of each word as he read along a piece of text. Signals (e.g., *then, before long, soon*) were no more important to him than other words. He was not "thinking through"; he was simply plodding along word by word, admitting that he would often reread the first few paragraphs of a selection four or five times, and then give up.

Boontan represents in the extreme the inappropriate expectations that children sometimes develop of what it means to read. His attempts to read, reread, and memorize were an unfortunate investment of energy, a prime example of a self-defeating strategy. It wouldn't have mattered how long Boontan persisted with the strategy he was attempting to refine; he would not likely have progressed as a reader.

Students like Boontan show why it is important to observe children on an ongoing basis for their perceptions about text. However, there are a number of guidelines that should be observed when choosing text for this purpose. First, text should be well formed and suitable for retelling. I have often found that teachers use selections from informal reading inventories (collections of "graded" selections designed to indicate children's reading levels) for children to retell. Most selections from these inventories are not designed for retelling at all—they are parts of larger selections so do not form a whole. Many pieces do not show sufficient connectedness to help the reader anticipate and connect one idea with another. In many selections, details are more important than bigger ideas. They have been designed to generate questions of a certain type from a relatively short piece. Asking children to retell such inappropriate text puts them at a disadvantage. I have sometimes asked graduate students to retell a third- or fourth-grade piece from these inventories, only to find that they are unable to do so without considerable stress. That should be convincing evidence that the pieces are inappropriate.

Following is a short lead-in to text that does not lend itself to retelling:

> **Bill and Shorty went to the woods. Bill was not supposed to leave the house. Shorty had homework to do. The boys went farther than they had ever gone before. Bill was getting worried. Shorty said, "Let's follow that trail...."**

The difficulty in retelling (and even reading) this kind of piece is that it provides no "think ahead/think back" clues. It is simply a collection of details made up of short sentences to make the text "easy" to read. If the text does not have these "think ahead/think back" features, the child who is retelling the piece is at a tremendous disadvantage and is not able to show what he is capable of doing with real text.

The following lead-in gives the reader a better shot at retelling:

> **The spider is one of nature's most peculiar creatures. Indeed, it is different from all other creatures. First, it manufactures**

> its own home from a sticky silk that it spins into an intricate web. Not only is this web the spider's home, it also serves to catch its food when insects get caught in the sticky silk. Another peculiar feature is the spider's listening legs. The tiny hairs on its legs pick up signals...

The advantage of using a piece like this is that from the start the reader/listener gets a sense of what to expect from the text. It sets up expectations in the reader that are tested as reading or listening proceeds. Then it allows the child to use these expectations as guides as he rethinks and retells the piece. In other words there is a structure that guides thinking and retelling. In fact one of the significant things to observe is whether or not the child is aware of the structure in text. These guidelines about text wholeness apply equally to narrative text if it is to be used for retelling.

Second, there are guidelines that apply to settings for retelling that need to be taken into consideration, especially with narrative retellings. The true sense of story can be assessed only if the context for storytelling is a natural one. The directive "tell me what the story is about" invites no more than the typical response: "Well, it is about...and then...and then..." This kind of directive does not invite a storytelling response. In fact it does little more than provide a context for determining how many details and facts have been retained. As a result, it is erroneously assumed that the child responding to the directive lacks a sense of story wholeness and sense of character.

To invite a storytelling response, a context for storytelling must be created. This has to include, among other things, an audience that is likely to be interested in the story. That is very different from an audience wanting to know whether or not you know the story.

Classroom audiences, though responsive, are not particularly "special"—they are there for so many celebrations, an audience there by convenience. There are, however, other audiences in schools ready to hear a story. Consider the following:

➤ Invite an audience, preferably of younger children or highly interested adults, who has not heard the story before. The audience may be one person or a small group. Suggest rehearsing with a tape recorder with the exhortation: "Tell the story the way you are going to tell the story to your audience. Pretend that the children are with you as you tell the story."

There are advantages to having the child record two or three versions to determine whether or not he revises in the process of retelling.

➤ Have the child listen to a recorded story. Then have the child tape his retelling for the teacher. (Make sure the teacher is not present during the taping so that the child feels a reason to tell the story to the teacher.) The child must get the clear message that he is telling a story to someone who wants to hear a story, not to one who wants to determine how much of the story he knows.

➤ For some children, puppets, dolls, and stuffed animals constitute as real an audience as any human audience. It is certainly worth trying (especially with very shy children).

➤ Have a child rehearse a story at school for the purpose of telling it to a younger brother or sister at home who doesn't know the story.

A special word is in order for the many young children in our schools for whom English is a new language, children whose oral retelling capacities fail to reveal what they understand about what they read and what is read to them. These children need teachers who give them the leeway to develop creative ways either to supplement retellings, or to supplant them. The following example demonstrates one such instance:

> **Jessica came to Calgary from Poland seven months ago. Winn, her ESL teacher, knows that Jessica understands far more than she is able to express and far more than her classroom teacher believes Jessica understands. Together, Jessica and Winn have read Tomi Ungerer's *The Three Robbers*.[2] Jessica, unable to talk about the story in any connected sense, picks up a pen and eagerly sketches her perception of the story showing by arrows the sequence of events. (See the following illustration.) The drawing shows the three robbers in black capes and hats, one with a blunderbuss, one with a pepper-blow, the third with an axe. It shows clearly the events culminating in their decision to buy a beautiful castle to house orphans like Tiffany whom they rescued from living with a wicked aunt.**

A retelling would have revealed little about Jessica except that she is just learning English. Her sketch shows remarkable understanding: a demonstra-

[2] Ungerer, T. from *Swinging Below a Star.* Toronto: Nelson Canada, 1989.

tion for herself, her ESL teacher, and especially her classroom teacher. Interestingly, Jessica did more talking as an accompaniment to her sketching than she normally did during story response time.

Concluding Comments

To find out about what strategies children use in reading, provide a full range of instructional settings and materials. Obtaining information from running records is a more formal process often done in a more formal setting. Running records provide both teacher and child a window through which a range of strategies can be observed over time. Children's records, when organized carefully, provide important observational data guides for child and teacher, and also legitimate documentation that shows the public what is happening. These records contain useful information on individual children; they also give the teacher an overall look at class patterns of strategy development that can help her determine further instruction and selection of materials.

Poetry and reader's theater have traditionally not been used in assessment. There are many advantages to using them; some crucial information is available likely only by these means. With children who have experienced failure, these methods are particularly useful. And because the exercises are enjoyable, children need not ever know that they are being assessed.

Although fluency can be assessed with running records, it is of such importance that it warrants special attention. Some children may have developed many important reading strategies but simply don't have the means to read with ease or enjoyment. Unless their fluency is improved, interest and motivation are at risk. Fortunately the materials that we use to assess fluency are variable. They may well be materials that are used in everyday instruction.

Retellings have been used extensively to gather information about readers. Information from retellings may be of questionable value, however, if it has been attained in an unnatural setting or if the materials chosen don't lend themselves to retelling.

REFERENCES

Braun, C., and P. Goepfert. *Swinging Below a Star.* In Strategies. Scarborough, ON: Nelson, 1989; Evanston, IL: McDougal Littell, 1990.

———. *Dreams Go Fast and Far.* In Strategies. Scarborough, ON: Nelson, 1990; Evanston, IL: McDougal Littell, 1990.

Clay, M. M. *Becoming Literate: The Construction of Inner Control.* Portsmouth, NH: Heinemann, 1991.

———. *The Early Detection of Reading Difficulties*, 3rd ed. Portsmouth, NH: Heinemann, 1985.

———. *Observing Young Readers: Selected Papers.* Portsmouth, NH: Heinemann, 1982.

Goodman, K. S. "Analysis of Oral Reading Miscues: Applied Psycholinguistics." *Reading Research Quarterly* 1 (1969): 9-30.

———. "Reading: A Psycholinguistic Guessing Game." In *Theoretical Models and Processes in Reading.* Edited by H. Singer and R. B. Ruddell. Newark, DE: International Reading Association, 1970.

Harste, J., V. J. Woodward, and C. Burke. *Language Stories and Literacy Lessons.* Portsmouth, NH: Heinemann, 1984.

Johnston, P. H. *Constructive Evaluation of Literate Activity.* New York: Longman, 1992.

Watson D., and P. Crowley. "How Can We Implement the Whole Language Approach?" In *Reading Process and Practice: From Socio-Psycholinguistics to Whole Language.* Edited by C. Weaver. Portsmouth, NH: Heinemann, 1988.

Conclusion

Looking, Listening, and Learning is about teachers observing children—looking and listening in particular ways to discover new insights into children's learning. Throughout the book I have argued that ongoing, intelligent kid watching—creative teacher observation—is the key to successful learning experiences for both teachers and children. Day-to-day observation helps to facilitate the integration of learning and teaching strategies and points the way to continuing professional growth. Specifically, the agenda for assessing children's learning has to be the undisputed domain of the person who has the greatest professional knowledge of the child—the teacher. Substantive educational change will not happen, however, as long as teachers have major positions of responsibility but limited authority over what they can teach or how they assess children's learning.

This book is also about *how* teachers observe and teach children. First, teachers must use observation to discover the foundations of literacy the children bring with them to school. Then, they must use strategies that build on these foundations. We know that children thrive on positive learning experiences. How they feel about learning and the enthusiasm they bring to the classroom depend greatly on the learning environment they create with their teachers. By cooperating—and being given a mandate to cooperate—with the students in the creation of learning environments that promote motivation and self-confidence in children, teachers contribute immeasurably to a child's long-term learning success, and to their own.

Index